ONE CABIN, ONE CAT, THREE YEARS

A Couple's Time in the Wilderness

ONE CABIN, ONE CAT, THREE YEARS

A Couple's Time in the Wilderness

David Marler

With Illustrations by Jeanne Marler

DCDESIGN BOOKS *Brattleboro, Vermont*

10 9 8 7 6 5 4 3 2 1

Printed in Canada.

A publishing imprint that acquires books that tell literary and compelling stories with a focus on writing about place. Visit www.greenwriterspress.com for more information.

DCDesign Books
Brattleboro, Vermont

ISBN: 978-0-9987012-5-7

COVER ARTWORK BY JEANNE MARLER.

Printed on recycled paper
in Canada at Friesens.

This book is dedicated
to the Quebec communities
of La Tuque and Lac-Édouard.

There is more to life than increasing its speed.

— MAHATMA GANDHI

Contents

Preface

IN 2013 MY WIFE, JEANNE, AND I—she in her late sixties, I in my early seventies—set out to fulfill our long-held dream of living in the woods for a year. Before leaving our home in the Eastern Townships of Quebec, I contacted the editors of *Tempo*, the monthly news magazine in the Town of Brome Lake (which I will refer to as "Brome"), to enquire whether they would be interested in receiving reports of our progress in the endeavour. They said yes. This book is based upon those articles and my daily diary entries.

My original intention was to produce a work echoing the objectives of Thoreau who, in addition to describing his daily life in his chosen wilderness, commented on the mores and politics of his time in *Walden*. However, each time that I penned such a commentary, I realized that it would detract from the essence and purity of our experience. The reaction to the *Tempo* articles proved that the unfolding of the tale of our daily lives was all that was required to engender intense interest and ample commentary. Thus, this memoir has to do exclusively with living in the woods.

Acknowledgments

I AM GRATEFUL FOR AND HUMBLED by the advice and assistance that I received from so many in the creation of this book: my sister-in-law, Marnie Reid Marler, for her proofreading; my daughter, Stephanie Martel, for her proofreading and comments upon the text; Monique Ethier-Yates, for her bilingual proofreading and special attention to the French; Ann Rajan, for her constant encouragement and suggestions on the subject of the methods of publishing; Kim Crady-Smith, owner of Green Mountain Books in Lyndonville, Vermont, for leading me to my publisher; Dede Cummings of Green Writers Press, whose enthusiasm for the book and eagerness to publish it turned my project into a reality; and the editor of this book, Michael Fleming, for his professionalism and patience.

However, there is one person without whom this book would never have existed, namely Jeanne. It is not just that the entire idea of living in the woods was hers, for without her I never would have reaped the rewards of the experience. She also read and reread my drafts of this book, and lovingly created the photography and artwork that illuminates it. She insists that it is I who wrote it, but I insist that the book is as much her creation as mine.

Introductory Notes

THE PROVINCE OF QUEBEC is French-speaking and, therefore, the majority of place names are in French. A lake is
un lac and a river is *une rivière*. These I have left in French;
hence Lac Tremblant, as opposed to Trembling Lake, or Rivière
Jeannotte, as opposed to Jeannotte River.

Measurements. I have used the metric system for distances and the
Celsius scale for temperature, but I've provided the equivalents in
both cases. I have not used the metric system for building materials, though. A two-by-four will, for me, always be a two-by-four.

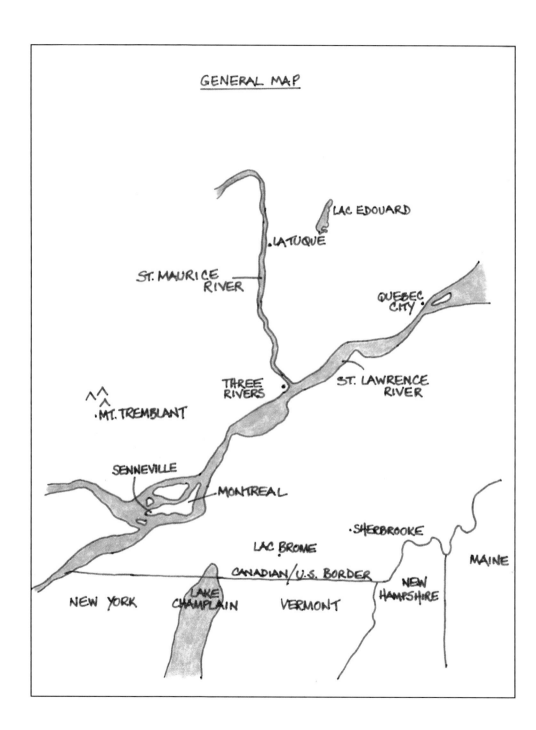

GENERAL MAP

LAC EDOUARD

LA TUQUE

ST. MAURICE RIVER

QUEBEC CITY

THREE RIVERS

ST. LAWRENCE RIVER

MT. TREMBLANT

SENNEVILLE

MONTREAL

SHERBROOKE

LAC BROME

CANADIAN/U.S. BORDER

MAINE

NEW HAMPSHIRE

NEW YORK

LAKE CHAMPLAIN

VERMONT

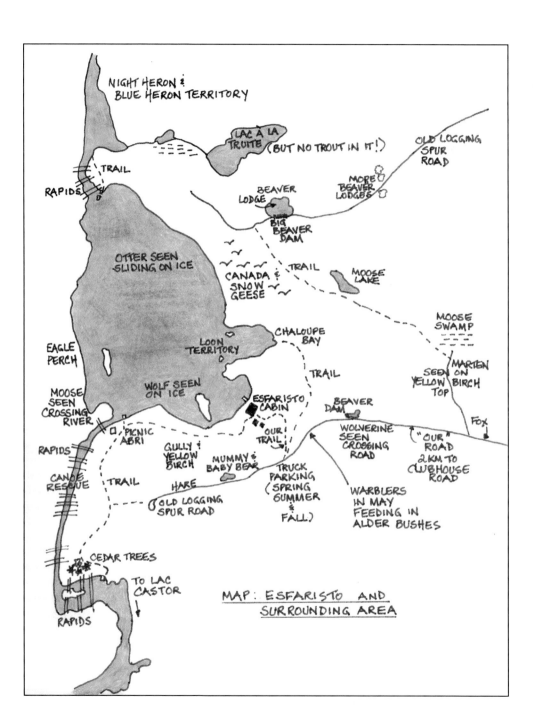

NIGHT HERON &
BLUE HERON TERRITORY

LAC À LA
TRUITE
(BUT NO TROUT IN IT!)

OLD LOGGING
SPUR
ROAD

TRAIL

RAPIDS

MORE
BEAVER
LODGES

BEAVER
LODGE

BIG
BEAVER
DAM

OTTER SEEN
SLIDING ON ICE

TRAIL

MOOSE
LAKE

CANADA &
SNOW
GEESE

MOOSE
SWAMP

EAGLE
PERCH

LOON
TERRITORY

CHALOUPE
BAY

TRAIL

MARTEN
SEEN ON
YELLOW
BIRCH
TOP

MOOSE
SEEN
CROSSING
RIVER

WOLF SEEN
ON ICE

ESFARISTO
CABIN

BEAVER
DAM

FOX

OUR
TRAIL

PICNIC
ABRI

RAPIDS

GULLY &
YELLOW
BIRCH

MUMMY &
BABY BEAR

WOLVERINE
SEEN
CROSSING
ROAD

"OUR"
ROAD
2KM TO
CLUBHOUSE
ROAD

CANOE
RESCUE

TRAIL

HARE

TRUCK
PARKING
(SPRING
SUMMER
&
FALL)

WARBLERS
IN MAY
FEEDING IN
ALDER BUSHES

OLD LOGGING
SPUR ROAD

CEDAR TREES

TO LAC
CASTOR

MAP: ESFARISTO AND
SURROUNDING AREA

RAPIDS

ONE CABIN, ONE CAT, THREE YEARS

A Couple's Time in the Wilderness

Cabin Esfaristo.

How It All Began

❧

WE ARRIVE IN THE MID-AFTERNOON OF JUNE 25, 2013. The car and trailer are loaded to the gills, and Scooter, our cat, lies sedated in her carrier. She does not like to travel and hates being confined. In particular, she does not like the movement of the car when we go over any sort of bump— but bumps are inevitable on the thirty-five kilometres (twenty-two miles) of unpaved forestry roads we take once leaving the highway in La Tuque. The unloading of our stuff and transportation to the cabin is a major effort. The parking spot on the track, a long-disused logging road, is 350 metres (382 yards) from the cabin. I make ten trips to the cabin, totaling 7,000 metres (7,655 yards), half of them loaded with packsacks, boxes, and bags. We've decided that, to be true to our wilderness endeavour, we will not have a road cleared to the cabin. The ground is too rough even for an ATV (all-terrain vehicle). In fact, three of them were wrecked during the building process. The carrying of immediately required articles and food accomplished, and Jeanne having begun to stow things away, we then indulge in a soothing swim in the river at the foot of the slope running down from the cabin and return to the cabin as enthused and as excited as newlyweds. We open a bottle of wine on the west-facing porch, watch the

Oil Painting, *Loons*, by Jeanne Marler.

sun set, and rejoice to see a pair of loons on the lake. Supper, then bed, exhausted but exhilarated.

For about as long as I have known Jeanne, she has wanted to spend an entire year—three hundred and sixty-five consecutive days—in the woods. This is not motivated by a desire to be a hermit or because she is antisocial. To paraphrase Montaigne, she is quite content living a private life, but that does not mean that she is unsuited to a public one. After all, she insists, it is only for one year. When I've asked, "Might it be that you would never come back?" she has answered, "It's only for a year." I should immediately add that this was not to be a year alone. All along, Jeanne has insisted that I am part of the plan and am to go with her. I like to think that this is because she loves me, but if that is only part of the reason (for she will need a hewer of wood and fetcher of water—a man servant in the general sense), then I am content, for I too need looking after and our lives have been interdependent since the first day of our marriage over fifty years ago.

Our adult lives have been outwardly quite normal—mine as a lawyer, hers as a choreographer, performer, and teacher of dance, first on the teaching staff of les Ballets Jazz de Montréal, then as owner of Le Centre de Dance Jeanne Marler, which included an annual, international, two-week dance seminar with a closing performance, called Focus on Jazz, that attracted aspiring pre-professionals from around the world. Then she was an interior designer with a diploma from the New York School of Interior Design; then the owner and operator of Camp Aeolian, a children's performing and fine-arts camp set in the pristine hills and woods of Vermont; and for the last twenty years or so, an artist. Jeanne has recorded the lives of our family with her camera and paintbrushes.

"But why in the woods?" many asked us. Most Canadians think of going south rather than north for vacations or retirement. Jeanne alone might properly be able to answer that question. She is a spiritual person, very much in the Celtic tradition. When we go to the woods she becomes very quiet. On family vacations to wilderness locations, the children used to say, "That's it for talking to Mum. She will turn into a rock or a mushroom or something for as long as we are here." And so it was. Upon our departures from such places, she often cried. We would ask, "What's the matter?" There would be no answer. I think it had (and has) simply to do with leaving places where her spirit finds its natural home.

For me, the pull of the Canadian wilderness is perhaps a combination of the experiences of my early childhood coupled with the books about Canada that my father gave me to read after we moved to England in 1949. During the war, while my father was ferrying Canadian- and U.S.-built planes across the Atlantic to Britain in the Ferry Command, my mother, my elder brother, Michael, and I lived in Shawbridge, Quebec, at the Shawbridge Club, and at other times as paying guests in the home of Mrs. Rushton-Woods. What I remembered of Canada was the smell of the Laurentian woods, the snow that covered the ground for the better part of six months of the year, and the crispness of the air. That all comes rushing back to me whenever I venture back into the woods of the Laurentian Shield, that part of eastern Canada that lies to the north of the St. Lawrence River, a place of rock, water, and trees, and long, serious winters.

I returned from England in 1959 to attend Bishop's University in the Eastern Townships, a region of Quebec, south and east of Montreal, that extends to the northern boundaries of the United States from New York to Maine. The Townships are beautiful and are among the most wonderful places that one might be privileged to call home. However, they do not have for Jeanne and me that rush of excitement and sense of wonder that envelops us when we are in the woods of the Laurentian Shield. At Bishop's I hankered for an invitation from one of our family's friends to go back to those woods, and when the invitation came from the MacDougalls to spend a weekend with them at Lake Anne, it rekindled that feeling which had slumbered within me for the decade of my upbringing in Britain.

At McGill, where I enrolled, following graduation from Bishop's, in the Faculty of Law, I met Ray Lawson. We became good friends. He owned a log cabin on Lac Tremblant, some 150 kilometres (about 100 miles) north of Montreal, in the days when it was remote, a pioneer's paradise. After law school Ray went on *le grand tour du monde* and he asked Jeanne and me if we would look after his cabin. We accepted without hesitation. How lucky we were. His grand tour took two years, during which time we took every opportunity to go to Lac Tremblant and revel in our wilderness adventures in the area's mountains, forests, lakes, and rivers. We paddled our fifteen-foot Chestnut canoe into every bay, nook, and cranny of the lake, dreaming of how wonderful it would be if we could ever afford to buy property on the lake, where we would build a log cabin.

Sometimes dreams come true. I came into a small inheritance. At the time, Jeanne was working as a teacher at West Hill High School in Montreal, the vice-principal of which was Archie Church. One day we saw an advertisement in the *Montreal Star* for the sale of land on Lac Tremblant, with the contact being "A. Church." The next day at school Jeanne asked Mr. Church if he was the "A. Church" in the ad. He was. Ninety acres of land with 2,000 feet of waterfront was for sale at exactly the amount of my inheritance, $5,000. That was in 1967. Today the same property would be worth many, many multiples of what we paid. My father gave me another $2,000, and with that and much sweat expended by me and by my friends, most of whom did not return for a second time, I built a log cabin. Jeanne and I imagined, however unrealistically, that one day we would live there permanently for a year or maybe more.

Our dream of living at Tremblant was shattered one winter night in the late seventies by the sound of snowmobiles on the frozen lake. Night after weekend night our paradise was invaded by those infernal machines, and in the summer, the size and number of motorboats began to increase. Floatplanes used the lake for takeoff and landing practice. Previously, canoes and small outboards had been used to transport families from the end of the road to their cabins on the lake. By the late seventies, however, the modern Tremblant had been discovered. As president of the lake association and secretary-treasurer of the Municipality of Lac Tremblant Nord, my weekends and vacation life became one of fielding complaints, drafting bylaws, and holding meetings, all in a futile attempt, I eventually came to realize, to slow—or, better, to stop—the invasion of one of the most beautiful and, until then, unspoiled natural areas in the world. After much family discussion,

Above: Cabin built by David at Lac Tremblant.
Below: David, Jeanne, and daughter, Stephanie, 1971.

we made the very difficult decision to put our Tremblant property on the market. However, that decision did not end our dream of one day living in the woods.

In 1967, Richard Riendeau, a partner in the law firm to which I was indentured, invited us to visit a fishing club of which he was and remains a member. We eagerly accepted and soon spent a memorable weekend in the pouring rain. Our adventures included the wash-out of the road to Montreal, requiring us to return by way of Lac Saint-Jean and Quebec City, thereby adding 350 kilometres (some 220 miles) to the trip. He asked if I might wish to become a member of his club. I would have accepted, but at that stage of my career I was unable to afford the annual dues. However, ten years later our friend, Jamie Morgan, invited us for a weekend to his fishing club, which happened to be the same club to which Richard had once invited us. Jamie also asked us if we would wish to become members. I answered, "Yes, as soon as we have sold our property on Lac Tremblant." The property was sold during the course of that summer, and we promptly became members of what I'll simply refer to as "the Club." We had found, without knowing it then, the location for our year in the woods.

This was and is pristine wilderness populated by wild trout, otter, mink, lynx, wolverine, wolf, bear, moose, grouse, bald eagles, osprey, herons (great blue and night), and, of course, loons. It was the loons that came to define the eventual "Year." Jeanne wanted, one day, to be there when they arrived, when they left in the fall, and when they returned in the spring of the next year.

Jeanne's affinity with the woods was such that at one point she decided she wanted a personal retreat from the routines of her life. That retreat was to camp alone in the woods for a week, the location being on the river which runs through the territory of the Club. Jacques Fournier, the Club's guardian at the time, and our son Michael, who was then ten years old (and who spent weeks every summer with his school friend, Thian, at the Club, "helping" Jacques), portaged and paddled Jeanne down to the chosen location and left her there, but not before receiving Jeanne's strict instructions that she was not to be visited or disturbed. We, the family, and, I am sure, Jacques, waited with trepidation for the

Oil painting, *Upper Clubhouse,* by Jeanne Marler.

moment when Jacques and Michael would retrieve her, alive and well, which they did.

Our annual canoe explorations, in and around the territory of the Club, inevitably led to the discussion of where precisely in the territory we might live if ever that should come to pass. The Club has, in addition to the main Clubhouse, a number of cabins here and there on nearby lakes and rivers. However, they are not insulated and generally not in a condition to reasonably house one for an extended period of time. The Clubhouse is insulated and fully equipped, but it would not have been appropriate for us to move in on a permanent basis. However, there was one camp that the Club members never used, an abandoned moose-hunting shack. It was on one of the government-approved sites, on the shore beside the widening of a river between two sets of rapids and not on any path likely to be taken, except by the occasional hunter, for there is no reason to go there and nothing to do once one is there, unless one wants remoteness and a life connected to what nature provides.

And so, after much discussion with the Club's executive in 2011, we sublet the lot from the Club. The existing moose camp was fit for neither man nor beast other than hibernating snakes, mice, squirrels, and the like. It would be taken down and our cabin built in the same general vicinity on a high and dry piece of land, facing southwest on a heavily wooded slope that leads down to a bay in the river. The higher land behind the site, as with all higher land in the region, is forested predominantly with yellow birch, locally referred to as *merisier*, an excellent hardwood for stoves.

I commenced clearing the lot in the summer of 2011 and continued whenever I could get away from the office in the fall of the same year. The cabin was to be built of logs from the site and constructed in November and December of that year by the Club's guardians, Roch Lepage and Paul Bérubé.

Building Esfaristo, November, 2011.

Building Esfaristo, December, 2011.

Building Esfaristo, January, 2012.

Building Esfaristo, March, 2012.

Finished cabin, December, 2014.

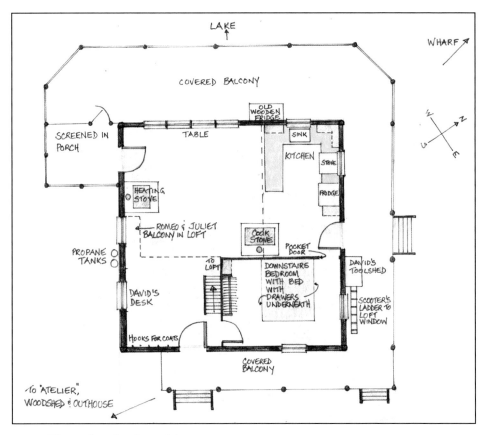

Floor plan for the cabin.

2

Building the Cabin

THE DESIGN OF THE LOG CABIN was inspired by the cabin at Tremblant and by Jeanne's study of feng shui. "Tremblant" was 5.5 × 10 metres (18 × 26 feet) and, with its loft, it was adequate to accommodate Jeanne, me, our two children Stephanie and Michael, and, from time to time, one or two guests. We believed that "Tremblant" could be improved by squaring the space to 7.5 × 7.5 metres (24 × 24 feet), and by increasing the ingress of exterior light by placing two windows in the eave on the south side, the loft to have a window in the north eave as well. The doors would be wooden-framed plate glass, one door leading to the utility area of the woodshed and the privy just beyond, one on the north front, and one on the south leading out to a screened-in porch. A 1.3-metre (4-foot) deck would run along the east side and continue under the extended overhang of the roof on the north side. A 2.5-metre (8-foot) porch would run along the west side overlooking the lake, with the screened-in porch on the southwest corner.

The trees were cut and debarked in November 2011, and the cabin was constructed as soon as a sufficient number of trees had been cut. I was surprised when Roch first laid out this procedure, because I thought that trees were cut in the spring when the

debarking process is very much simpler, the running sap effectively lifting the bark from the wood, and the logs then being
left for at least one year to season. Roch pointed out that no settler ever proceeded in such a fashion. The settler needed shelter
for the winter and that meant starting the process as soon as he
could. Further, Roch explained, although debarking is laborious
in the winter, the logs will retain their blond colour if building
is done in the winter, before the sap begins to run in the spring.
In addition, moving the logs from the place of their felling to the
building site in the winter permits them to be dragged over the
snow behind a snowmobile.

As with all differing methods, there are pros and cons. In this
case, the pro of the winter cut-and-erect method is exactly as
Roch explained. The con is that one is working in below-freezing
temperatures with wet logs, which are hard to handle and which
will shrink for at least two years. "And what," I asked, "about the
windows and doors? Wouldn't they be crushed by the shrinking
process?" His answer was that the logs will all shrink uniformly,
thus the spaces cut for the windows and doors will always remain
the same. I had never heard of this before but I can now tell you
that it works but also that it does require, until all has settled, some
adjustments to the door- and windowframes from time to time.

In December 2011, by truck and trailer (the truck kindly
loaned to us by Tom McGovern), we brought up the bulk of the
equipment: stoves, furniture, kitchen equipment, tools, etc., with
which we intended to furnish and equip the cabin, the object
being to allow us to use the cabin as soon as it was habitable. At
that point, though, the items could not be stored in the cabin as
it was far from ready to receive them and would not be until the
spring of 2012. In anticipation of this, Jeanne had shrink-wrapped
every item, big and small, because, apart from the woodstoves for
heating and cooking, which would be installed as soon as the
cabin was ready to receive them, everything else would have to
spend the winter in the snow and stay there until it melted.

Building with fresh logs in the winter also guarantees high
humidity in the cabin until they dry out. We experienced this in
spades when we stayed in the cabin for ten days in March 2012,

First stay, March, 2012.
Photo Roch Lepage.

Interior Esfaristo, March, 2012.

Interior Esfaristo,
March, 2012.

the bare cabin having just been closed in. The logs were, of course, frozen. As the warmth (I cannot say "heat") rose in the cabin, the logs gradually released their moisture. Water dripped from the ceiling rafters, emulating a leaking roof, and the humidity rose to 99 percent. Another challenge was lighting the fires and keeping them going. We had a paucity of dry wood.

Colin, Jeanne's brother, had given us a barometer as a Christmas present; it had a built-in humidity indicator. We were never able to reduce the humidity below 87 percent and it took until the seventh day of our stay to get the interior temperature up to 16°C (60°F). During our stay Roch came by snowmobile to visit us. Even though he did not say so, we were sure that he expected us to be ready to bail. But we were intent on staying the course. Had we given up at that point, would we have had the courage to embark on the real year in the woods? I must add that we did not have an outhouse at that time. Thus, for serious business I lashed a horizontal pole to two trees, approximately three feet above the place in the snow where one would place one's feet and squat while hanging onto the pole—this at temperatures consistently down around −20°C (−4°F).

There was never once an objection from Jeanne. Upon leaving, I asked her what she was most looking forward to by going home. She did not say a proper toilet. She said, "A hot bath." "And what about you?" she asked.

"Dry clothes and bedding" was my answer.

The completed cabin, which includes alterations effected in December 2014, has one corner of the downstairs squared off with interior walls and two doors as a bedroom. The two doors are required for the circulation of warm air into the bedroom during the winter. The rest of the downstairs is open. The corner adjacent to the bedroom is the back entrance, the other half of the cabin containing the kitchen, dining, and living space. The interior of the cabin has a partial loft covering its north and east sides, leaving the south and west sides (except, in the latter case, over the kitchen) open to the ceiling; this to allow the ingress of light to the entire cabin from the south-side eave windows. The loft contains a double bed, lots of storage space under the

eaves, and an art studio for Jeanne. Due to the height of the "un-lofted" portion of the interior, heat rises to the ceiling, thereby rendering the sitting area cool—an advantage in the summer. In the winter, this high ceiling creates a problem that is resolved, somewhat, by a solar-powered fan secured to the ridgepole in the centre of the cabin.

Downstairs bedroom, 2015. Below: New stairs to loft, replacing the ladder, 2015.

View from
David's desk,
2015.

View from
kitchen,
2015.

Kitchen, 2015.

Cook stove, 2015.

Speaking of heat, we have one good-sized cast-iron woodstove for heating and a very efficient woodstove for cooking. The heating stove is of the modern variety (although, as my tale tells, it was not so to begin with), which can be shut down and hold its fire for up to eight hours, thus not needing to be refueled during the night. In the winter, the outside daytime temperature is, generally, at least as low as −20°C (−4°F), falling at night to as low as −40°C (−40°F).

The toilet is a traditional, exterior one-holer, an immense improvement over the uncovered, hang-on-to-the-horizontal-pole routine. "What about the winter?" people have asked. That has never been a problem. For years we have been using outhouses in the winter without discomfort, and going to the outhouse at night is a wonderful way to see the stars, and to hear the ice groan and crack in the lake. A wooden seat, not a plastic one, is highly recommended; in the winter we remove the wooden seat and replace it with a piece of two-inch-thick styrofoam with a hole cut in the appropriate place. Amazingly, the winter seat never feels cold. Going to the outhouse is also the opportunity to return with an armful of logs for the stoves. That is why outhouses are always situated just beyond the wood pile.

Cabin showing position of woodshed, outhouse, and root cellar.

Our entire concept of "The Year" was to live as simply as possible. However, *simply* does not mean *uncomfortably*. The paraphernalia of modern inventions, perhaps required or at least desired
by a family in which both parents are working a full day, becomes
unnecessary when living is one's primary activity—a form of living that keeps one healthy, as it involves, in one way or another,
constant physical activity.

However, it was not just because the cabin had been built that
we could now embark on the life we had dreamed about—a life
of the great outdoors and all that it had to offer. We knew, of
course, that there would be learning curves, but there were more
than we had anticipated and I have to admit that at certain points
we became very frustrated, although at no time did we ever consider abandoning the project. The frustrations simply became
challenges which turned, ultimately, into the satisfaction of over-
coming hurdles in matters where we began with no expertise.
I came to accept that I was learning something by having to
deal with them. Jeanne has always been more tenacious than I've
been in such situations. For her, something which she does not
understand is a challenge to learn about it. For me, it was to call
for help. But here in the woods, there was no one to call: we were
just too far away. Addressing practical problems was not and never
could be a question, as it would have been at home, of calling the
electrician or plumber or some other expert, and, furthermore,
we did not want to do so. We had decided to embark upon this
adventure and now we had to learn how to deal with it.

Take for an example, and a prime one, the solar-powered electrical system. At the time of building the cabin, Roch and Paul
installed a small solar panel for the purpose of providing lights
in the cabin. This and its related electrical components were not
something that one can presume a lawyer and/or an artist to
know anything about, and we certainly did not. However, we
persevered, this requiring, initially, many unplanned visits to La
Tuque and beyond to discuss our situation and our problems with
the experts. Eventually, we did come to understand the system
(at least somewhat) and how to deal with such problems as arose,
problems which initially seemed to be insurmountable. As an

example, we had two electrical systems in the cabin, DC (direct current) and AC (alternating current). I think that I was taught something about this at school, but at the time it was nothing that I thought it would be useful to know. At the cabin, we learned to turn off anything connected to the AC system if we were not using it: for example—telephone, computers, radio, and lamps. If we did not, there was a constant drain on the solar batteries. Also, we learned that if we needed to run the generator we should plug it in directly to whatever apparatus we were using, so that the solar batteries were not brought into play. There is a warning light on the solar system which, when it turned red, indicated that the batteries were being seriously stressed. When that light came on, Jeanne would scurry around turning things off, while I ran outside and started the generator so that it would recharge the batteries.

In time, our initial extreme frustration gradually gave way to satisfaction—and the thought of "Who can we call?" diminished and eventually disappeared. This awareness that I could manage these problems, if I just calmed down and put my mind on them, did not, however, deter us from our resolution to keep things as simple as possible by doing manually all things of which we were physically capable, such as fetching water from the river by hand, rather than pumping it up.

Eliminate the unnecessary was the rule of thumb by which we chose to live. We did make some concessions to feasibility and convenience. A propane stove provides a quick surface heat and a hot oven when required. A wood-fired cookstove, on the other hand, serves also to heat, something which one does not want on a hot summer's day. Thus, the propane stove was rarely used except in the summer, because at the other times of the year the woodstove was always hot. What's more, a wood-fired cookstove is superior in performance to any gas or electric model. Many of our guests to the cabin had never used one and had no idea of its concept, thus giving me the opportunity to explain how it works. A woodstove's cooking surface is flat and is entirely heated, but not uniformly. The firebox is under the cooking surface on the left side (as you face the stove). Thus, the left side will be

David, water brigade.

Water brigade.

the hottest. From there, moving to the right, the heat gradually diminishes. Therefore, rather than having to adjust the heat under any pot or pan by raising or lowering the heat with a knob, one simply slides the pot along the surface: to the left to find more heat, to the right to find less. And one does not need a toaster. Toast is made by placing the slices of bread right on the surface, again moving them left or right, depending upon the level of heat required.

As to keeping food cold, I thought about the old method of chopping blocks of ice out of the frozen river in winter and storing them in a sawdust-insulated ice-house—but I knew that this would have been beyond my physical ability. Thus, we installed a propane fridge/freezer, which in itself was a considerable task in that no truck could back up to the cabin. As with such, for us, insurmountable projects, Roch and Paul with an ATV accomplished the task of moving it from the truck to the cabin.

To provide cold storage in the heat of summer, we conceded that a fridge/freezer would be essential. (At other times, we could supplement the fridge by using the screened-in porch as a fridge or freezer, depending on the temperature.) Many readers may not have heard of a full-size fridge being powered by propane. However, we have been familiar with them ever since I installed one at the cabin we built at Lac Tremblant. If the electrical grid does not reach the location of the dwelling, then the propane fridge is the answer. It looks and operates exactly as do electrically powered fridges. Both kinds, of course, are machines designed to use heat energy to drive the circulation of liquid coolant, the one type receiving electrical energy, the other propane-induced heat energy, just like a propane-powered stove or barbecue. The electrical model is plugged into an electrical wall socket; the propane model is connected by a tube to a tank, in our case one of 100 pounds. There is, however, one major difference between electrical and propane refrigerators. With an electrical fridge, if there is a power failure, one is stuck until the power company fixes the problem (unless one has a sufficiently large generator standing by). For the propane model, though, continuous operation is simply a question of making sure that you do not let the propane tank run dry.

For us, this means that we must always have reserve tanks stored under the cabin. I learned to stock up in the winter for the spring, summer, and fall, for it is only in the winter that I was able to transport the tanks to the cabin, because in the winter I could do it by snowmobile and sled. (And in case anyone is thinking of solar power, forget it. One would have to have an industrial-size solar setup to deal with the requirement of the full-size refrigerator and be constantly running the generator.) We buy the propane at Dubois Propane in La Tuque, where the tanks (two per trip) are loaded into the back of my truck, to be unloaded later into the sled of the snowmobile.

I will not deny the many times we wondered if we had lost our sanity in embarking upon this endeavour, which involved many hours of discussion, planning, and uncertainty. However, the dream, as you know, was not a sudden idea. It had been nurtured over decades. And so when the time for our taking up residence finally arrived, there were no second thoughts, only eagerness and the excitement of making the move into our new residence, a remote cabin in the woods which we playfully call "Esfaristo"— the Greek word for "Thank you."

3

Summer 2013

June 26, 2013. Picking up from my diary entry of June 25 [which I inserted at the very beginning of this memoir and in which I recorded our arrival on the first day of our adventure], I unpacked my clothing and then made more trips to and from the car to bring down the garden plants (tomatoes, parsley, chives, mint, rosemary, tarragon). Jeanne unpacked boxes and started to organize where everything should go, an enormous undertaking. Black flies were omnipresent and at cocktail time drove us indoors from the porch.

June 27. A night of terrific thunderstorms. I continue to unpack. The number of boxes is diminishing. Scooter is settling in. As each box is opened there is something for her to investigate and mark.

June 29. With everything soaking wet, it was a good day to pick up and start to burn the piles of construction debris which surrounded the cabin. I then laid out on the balcony all of my carpentry and other tools in order to determine the size of the toolshed I would construct. Until then everything had been crammed into the woodshed. At 17:00,

I felt that I deserved a break . . . fishing! I paddled up the river to the Echo Rapids. On my first cast, bang—a strike. For forty-five minutes, strike after strike, releasing the little ones that were hooked but keeping two half-pounders for the morrow's breakfast.

On the river, we only use flies. We feel that lures, worms, and other apparatuses would be too oppressive on the fish stock. We also de-barb our hooks so that the fishes' mouths will not be damaged and we can release them in an uninjured condition.

June 30. Raining. Built the toolshed. Highest temperature from June 26 to June 30: 18°C [64°F]. Lowest: 10°C [50°F].

July 1. Mist rising off the river in the early morning. Clear sky. Scooter ventured outside for her first excursion into the wild. Swainson's thrush calling at dusk. Great blue heron winging its way from its nest in the bay to its fishing spot

David, by completed toolshed, June, 2013.

David, returning from fishing, June, 2013.

Swainson's Thrush.

on the river. Swimming every day. The loons have been cruising and diving on the river.

July 5. Scooter has settled right in. She spent all of last night outside.

We installed a cat door into the window in the eave on the north side of the cabin and I built a platform outside the window from which Scooter could survey the world. Paul built her a ladder by which she could descend from and ascend to the platform. This arrangement avoided our having to constantly open and shut doors to accommodate Scooter's whims of when she wanted to go out and when she wanted to come back in.

Two half-pounders caught for tomorrow's breakfast. A glorious relaxed evening on the porch celebrating our good fortune.

July 6. Scooter's first kill: a baby hare, deposited on the balcony.

Scooter's ladder.

On this same day, I started to design a dock. We had been wading into the water from the shore, but the bottom was rocky and uncomfortable on bare feet. I wanted to be able to do a shallow dive into the deeper water. That would mean a ramp of four metres (twelve feet) in length. This was a job for Roch and Paul. We were hoping that the relatively well-sheltered bay, in which the dock is situated, would protect it from going down the river in the spring breakup.

Starting in the summer, bugs notwithstanding, made for an easy introduction to the venture. As for the bugs, Ray and Louise Hession had given us mosquito-net head covers. The black flies were horrendous from late May to the end of June. The mosquitoes joined them in force in mid-June and are now, mid-July, on the wane, replaced by deerflies. By late July the menace will be all but gone. There are those who can tolerate this seasonal horror

Jeanne, in her mosquito netting outfit. Photo David Marler.

and those who prefer not to. I am one of the former. Jeanne is of the latter. My activities tend to be out-of-doors and, at least for the time being, Jeanne has been busy indoors unpacking, organizing, and luxuriating in the realization of her dream.

"The Year" is very much Jeanne's dream. I am an enthusiastic and privileged supporter. Thus, I think it appropriate as part of the "why" to let you read her diary entry of July 10, her permission having been obtained.

> *This morning it happened. A lifelong dream came true. It was David who noticed them: our pair of loons drifting silently in the bay before our cabin. We had not seen them together since we arrived and now they seemed engaged in a reflective, loving interlude of their summer season in the north. Out with the binoculars and, lo and behold, the miracle of life's renewal. On the back of one of the pair were two little, fluffy balls of feathers. I'd seen photographs of this phenomenon of the chicks hitching a ride and had hoped that one day I would see the real thing. I shall do my yoga tonight with humility and gratitude.*

Adult loon with two chicks.

July 11. The loons provide constant diversion. The chicks are swimming solo with Mum close by. Dad stands guard, the main threat to the chicks being birds of prey, particularly bald eagles. We watch enthralled. We live as grandparents, worrying for the sake of the loons and their chicks in this predatory environment. The first indicator of an attack is the warning cry from the male loon. The chicks scurry to the side of Mum. In the early part of the season, the chicks are covered in downy feathers so that they will not sink and drown. They are like corks for the first few weeks and, because of their buoyancy, cannot dive; as a result, they are very exposed. Soon, though, they do learn, and the danger diminishes. The loons have an ally in the male gull defending its own nest. It will fly directly at the predator, thus distracting it. This activity allows Mummy and the baby loons to seek the cover of the edge of the river. The male loon joins in the retaliation to a degree but is mindful of the location of Mum and the chicks. He keeps up a continuous series of calls.

In the fall, the adult loons leave to go south to the Atlantic Ocean for the winter and they do this before the offspring, which stay on the river even as it freezes around them. Eventually there is only one patch of water left and when that day arrives we have become accustomed to a solitary cry, which we take to be a loon saying "good-bye," for after that they are gone.

July 12. Some 12 kilometres (8 miles) downstream, the river enters another widening.

It was on the shores of this widening, called Lac Castor, that the earliest camps were built in the latter part of the nineteenth century. All but one of these were very rustic and have largely remained so. It was in these cottages (*cabins* would be a more appropriate name for most of them) that Jeanne and I first experienced the territory with the Riendeaus in 1967. These cabins were erected by or for the first members of the fishing club. As with our structure of today, there was and still is no electricity and no running water, the toilet being an outhouse.

I mention this against the date of July 12 for the reason that Bob and Dan Newton, son and grandson respectively of the earliest Newton to sojourn on Lac Castor, came to visit us for supper. Their journey to us was quite different from the journey they would have made in those early times, indeed until the mid-1980s. This time the Newtons came by the forestry roads for the supper occasion. It was a memorable evening. Bob, who died in 2016, was a fund of the history and lore of those pioneering times. We built our cabin with a respect for those earlier ways and values. Let me describe how they would have arrived at their "camps" in those early days, and how they would have ascended the river to get to our location.

In those times, the Club's members would take the train from Montreal to a whistle-stop called Linton Junction, on the Lac-Édouard line. They would be met by the club's guardian, arrangements having been made by telegraph, and then ferried across the Batiscan River where, on the other side, they would scramble aboard a "scooter" at the railhead of a spur line originating in La Tuque. (A scooter is that type of conveyance that could be propelled along railway lines, whether by hand or motor.) About an hour or so after alighting from the train, the party would arrive on the south shore of the Rivière Jeannotte and be ferried across it to the north side, where was situated the Lower Clubhouse, the seasonal abode of said guardian, which was equipped with bunk beds for the members to accommodate an overnight stay. In 1958, the rail line was torn up and the rail-bed then became the route by which members, by automobile, accessed the Lower Clubhouse but from the opposite direction, i.e., from La Tuque. They still needed to be ferried across the river as in the railroad days.

Whether in the rail or automobile days, after their night at the lower clubhouse, the party, assisted by the guardian and the guides engaged for the occasion, would climb into canoes and paddle or be paddled, with one portage, some five miles up the river, to Lac Castor, where they would base themselves in their cabin(s) for the duration of their stay. There were and are a number of trout lakes in the vicinity which could and still can be accessed by portages with canoes. An entire day might be spent on such excursions, starting at the crack of dawn and finishing in the twilight of the evening.

In addition to enjoying these "local" excursions, truly enterprising members could ascend the river to where our camp is now situated and continue on to the Upper Clubhouse. Such ascents were excursions of heroic stature, for one was proceeding upstream and thus against the current. I use the word *proceeding* because the many shallows and rapids required one, in many locations, to pole, rather than to paddle, and to carry the canoe over six portages of varying lengths to arrive where we are—eight if heading for the Upper Clubhouse. All of this Jeanne and I experienced with Stephanie and Michael and our constant companion, Jamie Morgan, in the late 1970s and early '80s. It was by the rail-bed route from La Tuque that we first accessed the territory in the 1960s.

In those, for us, early days, Jeanne, the children, and I spent a winter week with Jacques Fournier at the trapper's cabin (the Club's at that time) behind the Lower Clubhouse. He organized snowmobiles for us to go from Lac Wayagamac, at the point where the road from La Tuque ceased to be plowed, a ride of some forty kilometres (circa twenty-five miles). Every day we would go out with Jacques to check his traplines, travelling far and wide on the snowmobiles. Jacques's principal, but not exclusive, interest was in beaver pelts. He would bring the trapped beavers back to his cabin and hang them outside, where they would freeze solid; in due course, once they were thawed, he would string their pelts on stretchers to let them dry. During that week, we were privileged to lead the life of a deep-woods trapper.

Over the years the methods of access had to be modified because the forestry companies abandon a forestry road once the cutting is complete in the area to which the road gave access. This has happened to us a number of times over the years and the most significant was the construction of Forestry Road 411, which connects La Tuque to Le Relais du Trappeur (henceforth

David, chopping stove wood.

Michael and Stephanie with a beaver taken from the trap line.

"Le Relais"), where we park our truck in the winter and which is linked by spur roads that bring us to our camp five kilometres (three miles) further on or six kilometres (four miles) if going to the Upper Clubhouse. (A *relais* is an inn. Thus, Le Relais du Trappeur is the place where a trapper can find a room and meals.)

Prior to the 411, access to the Upper Club was either by float-plane from Lac à Beauce, a village some five kilometres (three miles) south of La Tuque, or by continuing for an hour beyond La Tuque to the village of Lac-Édouard, where, prearranged by radio-telephone, the party would be met by the Club guardian in the Club's forty-horsepower boat and then ferried to the Clubhouse. Those trips were exhilarating, not always comfortable but always memorable, whether because of a sky filled with dazzling stars, or a rising moon, or a cold, rainy evening with a strong wind soaking us. The ride could take up to an hour in bad weather with contrary winds.

As I write, the future of the 411 is in question for the traditional reason, the cutting in the area it serves having been completed. Since this road was maintained by the forestry companies, a significant question arises as to who will pay for its maintenance now that the forestry operations have ceased in the area. The cottage owners who use the road for access to their retreats are insufficient in number to bear the cost, and I doubt whether the municipalities involved will agree to subsidize it. Perhaps that is as it should be. Are the days of the pioneers to be entirely eschewed for the benefit of those who desire ease of access to the woods?

And talking about the forestry roads, one of my concerns before leaving for the woods was whether our car, a Ford Escape, was rugged enough for what it would encounter. The 411 at its best is a constant series of shakes and bangs, with errant rocks and occasional washouts. Even without an actual grounding-out, I feared that the constant wear and tear would take its toll. On the other hand, with all the preparations for leaving for the north, the idea of having to involve myself in a vehicle purchase, not to mention the expense itself, held no appeal. My concerns were realized when, on July 9, I hit the ground with a significant bang while traversing the overflow from a beaver pond on our road, following which there came a disconcerting noise from the engine. The following day, July 10, I took the car to the recommended muffler garage in La Tuque, Garage Richer, to be told after an inspection that it was not the muffler but rather and more seriously a cracked main bearing; $5,000 was the estimate for repair. As I pondered this development and tried to sort out the options, I was looking out on the apron in front of the garage where there was a Toyota Tacoma truck with an "*À Vendre*" ("For Sale") sign in its window. Upon inquiry, Mr. Richer informed me that it was a 2009 model belonging to his son Denis, who needed a larger car with more passenger space for his growing family. The price was $19,000. I bargained this down to $17,000, less $5,000 which Mr. Richer offered me for my Ford Escape.

Although I knew that the minister of finance, Jeanne, would not be pleased, I was confident that the decision I had made, albeit without authorization (our communications systems at that point having not yet been installed), would receive approval. Jeanne had not enjoyed the punishment that the Ford was receiving, a punishment which the Tacoma was built to withstand.

July 13. Today our satellite dish was installed, which brought to us the internet and the telephone, high-speed and clear reception, just as if we were sitting at home, except for the phone on days of severe rain-, thunder-, or snowstorms.

The entire system cost $4,000, including installation, the original solar panel installed by Roch and Paul, the larger panel subsequently added, the satellite dish, the batteries and other necessary accessories, and the telephone. We pay no line fees to Ma Bell and no long-distance charges for calls within North America, and we pay $600 per annum for the satellite connection. I wonder why such a system is not used universally. Do we really need all these proliferating cell towers?

Before embarking on this adventure I had decided that I would eschew all mechanical tools, as did William Coperthwaite (*A Handmade Life*) and Scott Nearing (*The Good Life*). However, I was not completely successful in adhering to this idyllic notion. I could not avoid the generator if we were to be able to communicate with the outside world. Sufficient sunshine to charge the solar batteries is by no means a given, particularly in the months of November, December, and January, when the trajectory of the sun barely clears the treetops. Having some reliable method of communication with the outside world was required if we, our family, and friends were to sleep comfortably.

In addition, Colin, who gave us the barometer, also gave us a one-time satellite beacon emitter which would register at the Royal Canadian Air Force (RCAF) base in Trenton, which had on file our GPS coordinates and the coordinates of our outside contacts: daughter Stephanie, son Michael, and Roch Lepage.

As for a chainsaw, it was required because of the constant need to manage our wood supply.

July 14. Made a small 8' × 4' herb garden near the cabin and planted parsley, chives, tarragon, rosemary, and chervil.

I also made a start on the preparation and construction of a tent platform. I felled and de-barked two medium-sized balsams

Wood supply, spring, 2013.

to provide four ten-foot beams to be the foundation to the ten-foot-by-ten-foot platform. It became a hot day with a high of 29°C (84°F) which, what with the labour of the construction, led to three delicious swims in the now-warm river water.

July 15. I laid the platform beams with shims to level where necessary.

I would make the floor out of pine planks, eight inches wide, which I had brought up from home, they having come from a large white pine we had to fell for safety reasons. The pine was then made into boards by our Brome neighbour, Ronnie Raymond.

Construction of the tent platform.

The temperature rose to 31°C [88°F] today, and sitting on the balcony with our cocktails as the sun was setting reminded me of late afternoons on sailboats in the Caribbean.

Oil painting, *Sunset on the Jeannotte River*, by Jeanne Marler.

Until he reached the age of seventy-nine, my father spent his retirement on his multihulls exploring the Mediterranean, crossing the Atlantic, exploring the Eastern Seaboard of the United States, and eventually cruising in the Bahamas and the Caribbean. At various periods of my life I have been a very enthusiastic sailor, competing as a schoolboy in the U.K. and often taking our southern winter holidays on chartered boats. This enthusiasm transferred to both of our children. Stephanie, with her crew, Tom Egli, won the 2002 Fireball World Championships and was named Fireball World Champion Female Skip. Michael contested the local regattas in Senneville and Hudson, and at Cork (Kingston, Ontario). Jeanne loved the idea of sailing but was nearly always queasy. She was convinced, and not happily, that in my retirement I would become a sailing vagabond. Notwithstanding my many denials of such an intention, she did not dismiss her anxiety until she had me locked up in her northern woods adventure. Now I go sailing by reading the stories of other people's adventures. Some of them are horrific.

July 18. The mist was rising off the river and this boded another hot and humid day. I watched the loons feeding their young. Neither adult would pass a fish to a chick until the other adult had one ready for the other chick. Watching the loons is an activity of which we rarely tire.

July 19. Next week we will have completed the first month of our "Year."

July 20. A potential of violent wind storms forecast.

In the late afternoon we got it with a blow from the west that whipped down the river, blew away anything that was not firmly anchored or tied down and snapped the tops off some of the balsams. And so I had another pile of slash to clean up for an eventual bonfire.

July 21. A cool post-storm and unseasonable 8°C [47°F] at 06:00 this morning.

It was an ideal day for us to take our first walk in the woods, something delayed until this point because of Jeanne's aversion to the flies. Now they were starting to diminish.

This walk, which I named "the river round," became part of our daily routine. It involved walking up to where the truck is parked, then down to the river and along the river portage to the Club's picnic-shelter area, which was the site of Jeanne's personal retreat to the woods many years ago, then over to our camp, taking some fifty minutes in all.

July 22. 5°C [41°F] at 05:30. Thick mist on the river. Lit both fires, a first for the heating stove this summer.

Courtesy of the "net," we received a poem written by Dan Newton describing his early days on the river. Reading it was a trip down memory lane for us, recalling our adventures and escapades with Jamie Morgan and our children in the exploration of the area's every river and stream and the lakes which feed them. Nothing has changed in the intervening forty-odd years. The remoteness, the game, and the opportunity for adventure remain.

July 27. 5°C [41°F] 05:00. A perfect summer day unfolded out of the mist. A walk in the afternoon led to the discovery of ripening raspberries. Jeanne collected pearly everlasting to make wreaths.

July 28. 15°C [59°F] at 05:00.

By this date, my morning routine had developed: up at 05:00, light the cook stove and the heating stove, if required (which it has been for the past week), brew the coffee, write up the daily journal, clean up the kitchen, fetch wood to replenish the indoor supply, and fetch water from the river. Once all this has been accomplished, I check my e-mail in-box and by this time, about 07:30, there should be a stirring of my bedmate and the prospect of breakfast in half an hour or so.

August 1. Daughter Stephanie, husband Patrick, and their children, Daphne (9) and Cedric (7), have been at the Clubhouse, where we went to join them, the cabin not having been built to house six people and Scooter, and the Clubhouse is equipped with all manner of toys, board games, and, most importantly, the battery-powered fish which sings, over and over again, much to the delight of children, "Take me to the river, put me in the water."

The activities included: jumping, diving, and swimming from the Clubhouse dock, portaging and paddling to the picnic area, lunch, swimming off the rocks in the fast water and scrambling back up the rocky shore, portaging and paddling four kilometres (two and a half miles) back up to the Clubhouse, two carries (one of ten minutes, one of seven), fishing off the dock—hoping for a trout but catching only chub. Daphne did catch a nice-sized trout while trolling from a canoe, Stephanie paddling.

Daphne, Cedric, Patrick, roasting marshmallows.

August 2. Before breakfast Cedric and I picked raspberries and blueberries, and after breakfast it was time to say goodbye.

I felt distinctly sad and nostalgic as Jeanne and I paddled and portaged our way back to the cabin. The nostalgia was in respect of the many, almost identical, summer holidays, initially with Stephanie and Michael and now, some forty years later, with the addition of Daphne and Cedric, and Soline, daughter of Michael and Véronique. From the earliest of those times, our stays involved not only the fun of fishing and diving off the dock at the Upper Clubhouse, but always a full-day exploratory excursion. The excursions generally included much bushwhacking. They were considered by Steph and Mike to be forced marches. Now, I witness Stephanie and Michael instituting the same routines but with considerably less regimentation. The highlight of the excursions has always been and remains the annual canoe trip down the river.

August 5. We paddled and portaged to the Upper Clubhouse and then across Lac de la Grande Baie to "Jake's" cabin to pick blueberries. We returned with three quarts, only a fraction of what was there. The berries will be turned into a winter supply of blueberry jam.

Jake Eberts, a cousin of mine, loved this territory. His grandfather built the cabin on Lac Castor which he sold to Dan Newton's grandfather. Although Jake never stayed there, he annually made the downriver trip with the object of visiting the one-time family cabin. He became a celebrated producer of films, and his affinity for the woods can be found in his movies: *A River Runs Through It*, *Grey Owl*, and *The Education of Little Tree*. On Lac de la Grande Baie there was, in addition to the Clubhouse, a primitive trapper's cabin. Jake bought it in the 1980s and then renovated it, always maintaining its natural and unprepossessing presence on the spur of land upon which it sits. It was his retreat from the cutthroat and uncertain world of film production. He was a highly respected member of the motion picture industry, not only because of the inspired choice of his movies, but because of his integrity and modesty. It is because of that modesty that few, outside those in the industry, knew his name. As with us, Roch Lepage was the person upon whom he relied for all things which were beyond his capabilities. He died prematurely from melanoma in 2012 but not before he and many members of his family paddled down to us to see our cabin, then in the early stage of its construction. The remark I will always remember him by was his saying, on that visit, "*David, c'est un maudit bon camp.*" (That is: "David, this is a darn nice camp.")

August 6. Saw a red fox in the woods just above the river, and later in the day, when we went down for a swim, a mink. Woodpeckers (three-toed, black-backed, pileated, and yellow-bellied sapsuckers) active around the cabin all day. Loon family alive and well.

August 9. While shopping in La Tuque, I met a lady (whose name I subsequently learned was Mme Kathleen Bonenfant) in the office supply store, Megaburo.

Jake Ebert's (3rd from left) visit, spring, 2012.

Above: Pileated Woodpecker. Below: Three-toed Woodpecker.

Mme Bonenfant had lined up at the counter to pay for the photocopying which the store had done for her. I recognized the pile of copies to be of choral sheet music. As she turned to leave, I said to her *"Excusez-moi, madame, mais est-ce qu'il y a une chorale à La Tuque?"* ("Excuse me, madam. Is there a choir in La Tuque?") *"Bien sûr"* ("Of course"), she replied. *"La Brise du Nord"* ("The Breeze of the North") as if I should have known that. *"Est-ce que vous voulez acheter des billets pour notre prochain concert?"* ("Would you like to buy tickets to our next concert?") *"Non, madame,"* I replied. *"Ce n'est pas mon intérêt."* ("That is not my interest.") *"Vous chantez, monsieur?"* ("You sing?") she asked in a voice of anticipation. I answered in the affirmative. She asked, *"Dans quelle section?"* ("In which section?") I said, *"Basse."* ("Bass.") Her eyes lit up. *"On a besoin des basses!"* ("We need basses!")

Upon returning to the counter to pay for my purchases, the person serving me asked, *"Savez vous à qui vous veniez de parler?"* ("Do you know to whom you were speaking?") I said that I did not. She replied, *"Elle est la femme du maire!"* ("She is the wife of the mayor!")

August 13. Michael e-mailed to say that he and Soline would arrive that afternoon.

Soline and Michael, fishing off the dock.

He loves this place, its woods, lakes, and rivers. I am often reminded of what he said one day when he was, I think, about twelve years old. Stephanie, Michael, and I were in the car and Stephanie was talking about what she might like to do for a career. I asked Mike what he thought he might do. He answered, "I don't know what I want to do but I know what I won't do." "What is that?" I asked. He replied, "I am not going to get dressed in funny clothes and drive into a city every day, like you do, Dad." He has held true to that and is a vintner, owning, with his wife, Véronique, the renowned Quebec vineyard Les Pervenches. I mention this partly because that means he has very little time in the spring, summer, and fall to visit us in the woods, a place that was first and foremost to him in his childhood and adolescence. Now he grabs what little time he can to come up and renew his acquaintance with this wonderfully exciting world.

Michael, portaging.

August 15. This was the day of the annual down-the-river excursion, and what a day it was.

Serge Rosselet and his wife, Ruth, have a cabin on Lac Castor called Walboch, named after its first owner, Dr. Walboch of Boston. Lac Castor is the same lake on which the Newtons have theirs and is the lake upon which we had our first cabin, which we called Waldorf Castoria (the French word for beaver is *castor*). Jeanne and I loved the Walboch cabin and had once seriously considered that it might become our eventual home in the woods. However, it is on a peninsula of land and can only be reached by crossing water. We did not want to risk doing that in the winter.

Serge, his daughter Edith, Sandra (a friend of Edith's from Switzerland on her first visit to Canada; she had arrived at the Montreal Airport the day before), Mike, Soline, Jeanne, and I

(Ruth stayed back at their cabin to prepare supper) set forth from the Upper Clubhouse at 10:30 on a cool day in heavy rain. Rain does not matter on such excursions as one will inevitably be out of the canoe and in the river, at one point or another whether by accident or design. There are a number of rapids that can be shot but not always successfully, resulting in people being dumped in the river, and times when one has to get out of the canoe to pass over shallows. One is constantly exerting oneself in one way or another. Thus, one keeps warm, albeit wet—that is, unless one is, for whatever reason, simply a passenger, as was Soline, then too young to play an active role.

Jeanne, Soline, and I abandoned the excursion after the first hour or so and walked the shivering Soline back on the portage trails to our cabin, where we spent the day drying out, warming up, and playing games. At 16:00 we embarked in the truck with a canoe on the trailer and drove to Lac Castor, where we unloaded the canoe and paddled across the river to Serge and Ruth's cabin. What then transpired was a fascinating, international, multilingual evening, with sumptuous fare and, of course, fine wines from Le Vignoble Les Pervenches. The Marler contingent left at 22:00,

Oil painting, *Walboch Cabin*, by Jeanne Marler.

paddled back to where the truck was parked, loaded the canoes, Mike's and mine, onto the truck and returned Mike and Soline to the Upper Clubhouse, a fifty-minute drive from Lac Castor. Then Jeanne and I turned around to be back at our cabin at about 23:00, exhausted but exhilarated by the adventure and company. You might ask why they did not stay with us in the cabin. Well, they did for the first night of their visit, but the battery-operated singing fish resides in the Clubhouse.

August is the prime month to play, explore, and vacation in the woods of the Laurentian Shield. The weather is generally good and the water warm. The bugs have gone. The living is easy but can be made challenging, as on our downriver trip. Blueberry and raspberry picking is the prime activity at this time of year.

Guests were continuous at the cabin, including my cousin, Rob Paterson, who created and manages the *Tempo Blog*, which allowed for the continued dissemination of my *Tempo* articles.

Rob Paterson with David, blueberry picking, August, 2013.

Members were at the Upper Clubhouse. We enjoyed their company and their kindness in inviting us, on occasion, for supper.

August 22. Today I leave for Vancouver to attend the memorial service of a much-loved patriarch of the Marler family, Monte Marler.

This was my first departure of any length from the woods. I left with some trepidation, leaving Jeanne alone, but I knew that she would be quite content to have time for herself. Now that all communication systems were up and running, there was little need for me to worry. The one thing that specifically concerned me was Jeanne having to fetch water from the lake. The path down and back is steep and can be very slippery, and the buckets are heavy when full. Jeanne would have to be careful and bring up buckets half full. However, I had, to a degree, eased the water-fetching chore by hollowing out a log and attaching it to the eave trough, with the modification that I left the end open. This allowed me to catch rain water, which would flow out of the wooden extension and fall into strategically placed buckets. Jeanne was concerned about drinking water that had descended from an aluminum roof. (She is very health conscious in respect to every aspect of life, and very knowledgeable about diet. Lucky me.) But on rainy days we could at least use the roof water for washing the dishes, which reduced the fetch-water chore.

I returned from Vancouver on August 26, following a memorable family reunion. Jeanne had survived well. The cabin was spotless, with wine and cheese laid out for my reception. She told me that she had been extra careful in the physical aspects of life, principally fetching firewood and water and daily bathing in the river. Jeanne had been visited by Mark and Julie Barber and family, who had been at the Clubhouse. Mark is another member of a three-generation Club family. His father, Alex, now in his eighties, heads the clan. Alex never misses the annual spring and fall gatherings. Mark's son, Geoffrey, is a keen member in his own right.

August 29. 14°C [57°F] at 06:00.

The fishing would not be good for the closing weekend of the fishing season, which ends at sundown on the second Sunday of September. There was not now enough time left for the water to descend to a temperature (10°C, 50°F) at which the trout would become active.

This has much to do with global warming. It used to be the last week of August and the first two of September which would provide the most productive and exciting fishing. This ceased to be the case some fifteen years ago. Those who have become members more recently would, understandably, be suspicious of the tales of the catches in earlier times, except for the fact that the Clubhouse walls are decorated by cardboard cutouts of fish consistently in the three- to five-pound range, the earliest cutout being dated September 1938.

September 5. 2°C [33°F] at 07:15. The first cold morning but it will not be enough to make the fishing productive

Michael.

for Mike, who arrived yesterday afternoon.

It is at this time of year that he and I remember his first significant catch, a five-pounder, at the age of twelve. However, as much as the anticipation of a catch is what brings the fishing enthusiast to the water, it is the joy of being in or on the water, in the silence and solitude of one's thoughts, that is the memorable and therapeutic reward of the activity.

During his visit Mike saw a bear on the shore of the river. More remarkable and rare was Jeanne's sighting of a wolverine crossing the old road that leads to our parking place above the cabin.

I was absent (at the dentist) for all of this excitement but had the pleasure of returning to recuperate in our new bed, built and installed by Roch and Paul. In anticipation of the coming cold of winter and so as to provide more storage space, Jeanne had designed a bed the sleeping level of which is almost three feet above the floor. Underneath the

Drawers under our bed.

bed are large drawers which hold a significant amount of clothing and other things, including an alcove for wine which would otherwise freeze in the winter if stored on the floor. Admittedly, one needs to "climb" into bed and the floor seems a long way down when getting out of bed. Nevertheless, it serves its purposes well, allowing us to put the more conventional double bed, which we had been using, in the loft for guests.

September 6. 1°C [34°F] at 06:00.

We went to La Tuque to investigate snowmobiles. First, we consulted with Denis at Nautico, the Bombardier dealer, who advised for our needs an "Expedition," which, he explained, was the new and improved version of the "Skandic," known as being the workhorse of the Bombardier machines. We are not snowmobile enthusiasts, as the reader already knows. Since in the winter we will not be able to get the truck to its parking area above the cabin, we will need a snowmobile, like it or not, for transportation to Le Relais where, as previously stated, we will park the truck. However, we were somewhat taken aback by the price, $11,000.

On the way back to the cabin we stopped at *la barrière,* which is the security gate on forestry road No. 411, which we take from La Tuque to go to our cabin. One must stop at *la barrière* to register in and out and declare one's catch, in the case of fish, or take, in the case of game. We chatted, as we always do, with Richard Delisle, the guardian and the husband of Nathalie Bergeron, who is the secretary of the ZEC de la Bessonne. Both are a fund of knowledge about La Tuque and became frequently visited friends. They took us under their wings, guiding us in many different matters, including, to return to the subject, snowmobiles. Richard knew of a second-hand Skandic for sale at a nearby lake, asking price $3,000.

And what is a "ZEC"? It stands for "*Zone d'exploitation contrôlée,*" which more directly means an area designated for hunting and fishing in Quebec. ZECs range in size anywhere from some hundreds of square kilometres to a handful of more than 2,000 square kilometres. Historically and prior to the creation of the ZECs by the Quebec Government in 1978, the territories which the ZECs now manage were the exclusive domain of the private fish and game clubs. The private clubs employed wardens whose primary role was to patrol the premises and keep out any person who was not a member. Trespassers, called "poachers" in the fish and game world, were subject, if apprehended, to being summoned before the local magistrate and, if convicted, to paying a fine. Effectively, therefore, the average citizen, unless meeting the social profile of a club member and having the wherewithal to pay the dues, was excluded from entering the finest of Quebec's hunting and fishing territories. The new law did not abolish the private clubs but removed from them the exclusive use and control of the territories. The Zec de la Bessonne is the ZEC which we cross on the 411 in order to get to our cabin.

September 7. 1°C [34°F] at 05:00.
The temperature is not good news, from a fishing point of view, for the large group of members at the Clubhouse, but good

news for the current task at the cabin, namely caulking and staining the logs, a joint effort of Jeanne, Paul, and me.

We discussed with Paul the snowmobile question and he confirmed that a Skandic would be ideal for our purposes. And so, in the afternoon, we drove over to Lac-Émond to introduce ourselves to Pierre Lemire and his wife, Monique. After a most hospitable period of getting to know each other, principally talking about how we each had discovered the territory (this conversation aided by beer and munchies), we became the owners of the Skandic.

September 11. Went to my first choir practice.

Karine Hémond introduced the new choir members by their first names until she got to me whom she introduced as *Monsieur* David. Why *"Monsieur"* I asked, when everyone else was introduced by their first names only. She answered with a smile. I reflected that it was either because I was not from La Tuque, a tightly knit town where everyone knows each other or, perhaps, because I was some number of years older than anyone else in the room.

In that and many other respects La Tuque is a very conservative town. People of all ages are treated with respect, and this is reflected in the manner of their greeting. I came to realize that "Monsieur David" and "Madame Jeanne" was an indication of respect for age, not a coolness of greeting, and, frankly, I consider this formality to be something to which we could all usefully revert. In the course of my professional life, I receive countless e-mails addressed to "Dear David," and I used to instinctively think that the message must be from someone I surely know. It might be . . . but almost invariably it is not. Even the prime minister of Canada, Justin Trudeau, whom I've never met, addresses me, in the multiple missives I receive from the Liberal Party of Canada, as "Dear David." If I were to meet him, would I be expected to call him "Justin"? If I met the Queen, should I call her "Elizabeth"? I would be uncomfortable in doing either though less so the former. Even Nathalie Bergeron, whom Jeanne visits frequently, discussing all matter of things, has, with difficulty and following Jeanne's persuasion, changed from greeting her as "Madame Marler" to "Madame Jeanne."

La Tuque is a community that exudes welcome. It is a town where people will greet you as you pass them on the sidewalk with a *"bonjour"* whether they know you or not. The people in the stores and restaurants are always welcoming, the quality of service first-class and always with a smile.

Although La Tuque is the town which we visit regularly for our provisioning, for the annual art symposium where Jeanne exhibits, for the choir in which I sang for the first two years of "The Year," and where we were made welcome by so many, our cabin is actually situated in the Municipality of Lac-Édouard. It is another vast area of wilderness where one finds the historic and very special Village of Lac-Édouard, with a permanent year-round population of some 175 people. The village is notable, by reason of its isolation, as the location of the sanatorium built in 1904 to treat victims of tuberculosis, and as the place where one finds La Seigneurie du Triton, perhaps the most famous of the fishing clubs established in the 1800s. The members and their guests of the private club, as it then was, included the rich and historically famous, amongst many others, presidents of the U.S.A. and Winston Churchill. Le Triton is now and has been for many years a very upscale outfitter.

The sanatorium ceased to treat tuberculosis once antibiotics were discovered. It then served other hospital purposes, including the treatment of military veterans, but it was finally closed in 1982. More recently, a consortium of fruit and vegetable producers in the more temperate climates of Quebec conceived of utilizing the land of the hospital site as a location in which to grow late-season strawberries. This initiative went into production in 2013. The plan included an ambitious project of restoring some of the buildings of the hospital, most of which were falling down from lack of care, and expanding the agricultural project into a complete market garden production. Whether these projects will succeed remains to be seen. The season is short and the location very remote. But it is the dedication of this tiny community that makes the village so unique and which draws hundreds of non-residents to visit every summer.

Our first discovery of this magical place was the result, as I have already mentioned, of its being the way to get to the Upper Clubhouse in the early days of the Club. It was a long drive from our home, then in Senneville. One of the highlights of our annual family holiday trip to the Upper Clubhouse—for the driver of the car, but not necessarily its passengers—was the arrival at the turnoff road leading from the highway to the Village of Lac-Édouard. The access road was not paved in those early days and was, as it is today, a series of steep ups and precipitous downs, the type that, given sufficient speed, create the same sensation, one's heart in one's mouth, as does a roller coaster when it reaches the summit of its climb. I have already commented upon the boat rides from the village to the Club in those early years. Lac-Édouard and its citizens have a very special place in our hearts and in our memories. Living there is a thought which crossed our unpractical minds from time to time.

The days are closing in. Soon it will be dark for up to some fourteen hours a day. Although the daylight hours are filled with the fundamentally necessary basic activities of living, the hours of darkness would seem interminable if we could not read. Without our Kindles I think we would have gone stir-crazy. We refuse to have a television and have not had one since 1989, when we realized how much mindless time I (not Jeanne) wasted sitting in front of it. But I must admit that on my work-related sorties, I do indulge in watching the tube in whatever hotel I might be staying. It is enough to remind me that I do not want one in my home.

September 18. Coming back from choir practice in the truck, I caught a moose in my headlights.

This is rutting season. It will soon be moose hunting season. Caulking and staining the logs continues. A minimum outside temperature of 10°C (50°F) is required for staining. That window is slowly closing.

4

Autumn 2013

September 20. The summer birds, waterfowl excepted, have gone. Hummingbirds that entertained us at their feeder left yesterday. Geese are passing overhead daily. Migrating ducks are on the river. Loons, of course, are still here with the chicks strengthening their wings in anticipation of their eventual departure. Fish are coming onto the spawning beds. Temperatures are now mostly in the single digits [°C] all day.

September 25. We took the opportunity of a clear, windless day to paddle up to the Echo Rapids, following the shore there and back. We picked a bunch of bright red berries with crimson leaves. Upon our return to the cabin, identification indicated that they were wild raisins, possibly poisonous.

The shore is also brightened by the red berries of the American Mountain Ash, which grows here only to the modest height of some five feet at best. They seem to be equally spaced along the shore, as if planted in a garden, particularly in our bay, which faces south and west. The berries of this tree are edible. Squirrels, partridge, and gray jays rely on these vitamin-rich berries. (Readers

might, by now, be able to rec-
ognize where Jeanne's knowledge of such things is being
inserted.)

September 27. Saw a wolf
on the forestry road.

September 28. Exterior
temperature 4°C [40°F] at
06:00, interior 18°C [64°F],
proof that the caulking is
doing its job as intended.
Paul finished the staining
and caulking today. The

Mountain Ash berries.

high was 22°C [72°F]. Grouse hunters are at the Club.

Experience showed that two tanks of propane were sufficient
from late spring to mid-autumn. Thus, to be safe, say six cylinders
a year. The demand should be similar year-round, as we did not
use propane for heating, only for the propane stove and refriger-
ator/freezer. In the winter, we will be able to shift the cylinders
with ease, using the snowmobile. In the other seasons, we need
to ask Roch and Paul to bring them down by ATV from where
we park the truck.

Our love of this life made us reflect upon when we would
return to our home in Brome once "The Year" was over. We had
always thought that we would stay for the summer of 2014, but
what then? On September 29, out of the blue, we received a ten-
tative inquiry from a couple, Luc and Sylvie Robert, who were
born in Quebec but who have spent their entire adult lives in
France due to the husband's employment. They wished to re-es-
tablish Quebec residency. After an exchange of e-mails regarding
the details and a visit to the house by the husband, he signed a
year's lease, to commence in April 2014, when the lease, to the first
of our renters, would expire. The stars were aligned. Discussion
over. We were happily committed to being here for an additional

David, canoe excursion prep.

twelve months. It seemed to us that one year would have been far too short a period of time. We were preoccupied with learning to live full-time in the woods and were far from having completed the learning curve. Nor had we yet reached the winter!

October 4. A perfect warm and sunny day. A paddle in the morning to the Clubhouse to retrieve one of our life jackets for Jeanne, in anticipation of visiting the Newtons on Lac Castor this evening.

As it happened, we did not descend the river by canoe but went by truck to Lac Castor and paddled over. It was an epic evening, with Bob regaling us with the stories and tales of the early days.

While returning, after about fifteen minutes on the road we passed a truck coming from the opposite direction. What you may ask would be newsworthy of that? Nothing in itself, although seeing other vehicles at night on the road is rare. However, a

Bob Newton, on the porch of his cabin on Lac Castor.

few minutes later I decided that I should check the securing of the canoe. No canoe! It was not there. I turned the truck around and, feeling very inadequate, went back down the road looking for the canoe. I was not hopeful that we would find it in good condition, it being made of wood and canvas. Some few minutes later, again the headlights of another vehicle. Thinking that maybe its driver had seen the canoe, I prepared to flag him down. I did not need to. It was the same truck, this time with a canoe in the back—our canoe! You will understand why we have such confidence in the people who live in this region. He had taken the time to stop to load a canoe which he thought might be ours, turn his truck around, and attempt to catch up with us.

Inside the Newton cabin.

Oil painting, *Autumn Mist*, by Jeanne Marler.

We were now in moose-hunting season and keeping our heads down, wearing fluorescent orange covers whenever we went out. The hunters knew we were here and were respectful of that, as we were respectful of them. As the fall progressed we saw a number of moose, including a bull eagerly following a cow. We hoped that they all would live through the season but we knew, already, that some had not. We also saw, not fifteen metres (fifty feet) from us, a male partridge displaying its full magnificence, surrounded by five eager hens. We watched enthralled from not more than six metres (twenty feet) away, without the birds being at all distressed by our proximity. They had more important things on their minds. The fall colours were magnificent, the dark green spruces lining the shore of the river, with the orange and yellow glow of the birches, white and yellow, behind.

October 12. The tamaracks are now having their golden moment. The geese have been coming over daily for the last month. They are certainly not an endangered species. The trout are on the spawning beds right in front of our cabin, and in the evening the water is constantly rippled with their rises. The "baby" loons are still here. The parents will leave soon.

Loon parent and adolescent "baby."

There was, of course, much which we continued to do outside without snow, but were ready for it. We received our first fall of snow yesterday. My main activity was moving wood from the woodshed to the decks of the cabin in preparation for the winter.

October 14. Exterior temperature 9°C [48°F] at 05:00.

October 16. When returning from choir practice I was charged $4.50 for arriving after 21:00 at *la barrière*. The person on duty, not Richard, was not impressed by my community involvement. Rare exception to the usual tolerance of the people of La Tuque. Not to worry, moose season ends at the end of this week. From then until the opening of the fishing season in May 2014, there will be no one at *la barrière.*

October 23. 0°C [32°F] at 04:00. A sheen of ice in the bay. Roch and Paul installed an insulated chimney for the cookstove because it is too close to the bedroom partition wall. The heating stove's chimney, not insulated, stands well away from the log wall of the cabin.

October 24. Snowed all day. No accumulation.

November 15. A solitary loon called today. No modulations—sad and lonely calls. Was this the goodbye of the chicks?

November 17–18. River is now iced over except for a patch of open water below the Echo Rapids. I saw one loon chick in it on the 17th and the morning of the 18th. In the evening that solitary cry again and then no more loon.

I had work to do in Quebec City and Montreal and wanted to pick up something in Knowlton from Mike Royer, who had supplied me with many manually operated tools, i.e. those not requiring electricity. I had seen on one of my visits to his store an old wooden refrigerator, the type where one loads ice into a top compartment such that the cold air descends over the produce stored on the lower shelves. It was and is a handsome piece of furniture and I thought it would look fine on our porch and would serve as a freezer in the winter and for storage in the other seasons. The challenge was not so much how to get it to our parking area above the camp but rather how to get it from there to the cabin, and then, how to get it onto the porch. It is very heavy. Mike and his son had loaded it onto my truck in Knowlton with the use of a forklift.

On the morning following my return to the camp, I tackled the project of how to unload it. There was no way in which

Jeanne and I could move it from the bed of the truck. So I backed up the truck to a tree and roped the fridge to it. I then eased the truck forward, with Jeanne directing me, until the fridge had been pulled to the back of the bed, partly onto the tailgate. The challenge then was how to get it to the ground. Jeanne and I still could not move it manually. So I decided that Jeanne would drive the truck forward very slowly, inch by inch, and that I would guide the fridge down to the ground, as best I might be able. Jeanne does not enjoy adventures that tempt disaster, and the truck has a very sensitive accelerator pedal and a quick, powerful pickup, but I was determined to unload the fridge, particularly as it was now half on and half off the truck, and we would not be able to use the truck until we had unloaded the fridge. Jeanne got up into the cab, started the engine, and touched the accelerator. The truck leapt forward as do thoroughbreds when the gate opens. I threw myself into the ditch as the fridge flew off the back of the truck. It fell unaided to the ground, landing neatly, right side up, sustaining no damage. In a gymnastics competition it would have been awarded a 10.0 for dismount. Jeanne descended from the truck quite shaken by the experience.

The fridge remained at the parking area until Paul and I, witnessed by Stephanie, who was up for a visit with Daphne and Cedric, wrestled it onto the trailer behind Paul's ATV, and then wrestled it off below the porch at the cabin. I recall that we then lifted it onto the porch with Stephanie's help.

Stephanie, having read an early draft of this book, wrote to me as follows:

We did not lift it on to the porch. Up until this point I had not helped at all. I watched you and Paul in amazement as you tried to manhandle the thing. Worried that you would injure yourselves (Mom had decided not to get involved), I insisted that there was a better way. Being a woman and not predisposed to believe that I can lift anything, especially a large cuboid of a fridge up onto a porch one metre [just over three feet] off the ground, I suggested that you could fetch one or two boards to create a ramp and a lever.

Paul Bérubé, David and Stephanie with the antique fridge in its place on the porch.

We then gently slid the thing off the back of the ATV trailer neatly on to the porch. Clearly you did not learn anything from this if your diary entry states that I helped you lift it with strength!

Stephanie and her children were visiting because this year would have been the first time in her life that she and her family would not be celebrating Christmas with us, a matter of considerable regret for all of us. She took the matter in hand and, with Daphne and Cedric, made the trek to us from Thunder Bay for this November 18–22 visit. We stayed at the Clubhouse and made daily excursions on foot into the woods, including one which particularly impressed me, a walk from the Clubhouse to our cabin and back, a round trip of some ten kilometres (six miles).

When Steph and the children left, Jeanne and I were very sad to see them go. We were now alone in the woods, with winter descending upon us.

December 7. Jeanne's 70th birthday. Celebrated, chez nous, with a dinner of rack of lamb.

Christmas tree.

Oil painting, *Little Green Stove,* by Jeanne Marler.

December 10. We put up a Christmas tree, a small balsam which I cut from the side of our parking area. It will be a lonely Christmas without the family, but Christmas nonetheless.

Jeanne is a traditional Christmas card sender, a dying breed. The card has for years been a print of one of her paintings. We have learned that certain of our friends have framed the cards and hung them on their walls.

December 11. Our east-side deck needs a roof; otherwise the roof of the house will dump its snow load upon it. Paul arrived and I spent the day with him felling and debarking trees for the roof supports.

Paul is a very good teacher and is happy to have a novice helping and learning beside him. Amongst other things I learned that day was that to de-bark a tree in the winter one takes long pulls with the scraper, rather than trying to lift the whole of a section of bark with one pull, as one can do in the spring. To keep the log on which one is working steady, cut a notch in the stump from which it was felled and place the end of the log in the notch.

In very cold temperatures, a chainsaw may need choking for every start until it is warm. Even then one may need to flick the choke lever on and off before pulling the cord. In normal starting, one leaves the choke lever in choke position until the machine gives a sign that it will start, a little rumble. One then takes the choke off, pulls the starter cord, perhaps once or twice, occasionally three times, and away she goes. If one does not follow the right procedure the saw will inevitably be flooded and starting it will be next to impossible until the excess fluid has evaporated.

December 12. Roch and Paul at the cabin to put up the roof over the east-side deck. The exterior temperature never got above −28°C [−18°F] all day. I could not start the snowmobile. Roch and Paul gave me a lesson in

David, debarking a log.

cold-weather starting. Also the generator would not start. They told me to release the gas cap and/or play with the on-off switch.

December 15. It's warming up. I never thought the day would come when I would rejoice at a high of −16°C [3.2°F].

The deck roof is a great success. We can now walk around three sides of the cabin under cover. The roof will also keep rain and snow from coming into contact with the sill log of the east-side wall and direct the spring avalanche of snow and ice from the roof to beyond the deck. We learned, on our stay in March 2012, to be very conscious of the fact that at some point in the spring such an avalanche would occur. I am not sure anyone would survive if hit by it.

5

Winter 2013–2014

W E WERE LOOKING FORWARD TO WINTER. We spent much of the fall anticipating and preparing for its arrival. Snow arrived here on October 30 and built up to 7.5 centimetres (three inches) over three days and then melted away, but it's now back to stay. As of today, December 15, we have twenty centimetres (eight inches) on the ground. I had put a board up against a tree and marked it at intervals of one foot up to five feet. (I still measure snow depth in inches and feet). Overnight temperatures are now consistently below freezing, with the overnight low thus far being −35°C (−31°F) and a string of −30s this week.

The snow and cold provide us with another learning curve. Starting the snowmobile, starting the generator, starting the chainsaw, getting up on the roof to sweep off the solar panels, keeping open the hole in the ice from which we draw the water, staying warm in the cabin. However, the winter brings exactly what was anticipated and it is spectacular. The trees are laden with snow that is always white and fluffy because there is no thaw.

We now snowmobile the first five kilometres to Le Relais, where we leave the truck. From there it is forty-five kilometres to La Tuque for our shopping, which we do once every two weeks on Fridays because the forestry road is only plowed on

Thursdays—that is, if it is plowed at all. If we had to get out on any day other than a Friday it might conceivably be by snowmobile all the way and that would mean taking the dedicated snowmobile track, entailing a run of seventy-four kilometres, something which we have no intention of doing. Many of the recreational snowmobilers travel at alarming, indeed, reckless speeds, and, given that

Shoveling off the roof.

the snowmobile roads are not divided highways, head-on collisions occur, sometimes with fatal results. We were never at ease when travelling to and from Le Relais on the snowmobile and we are sure that these two old fogies creeping along caused frustration to those obsessed with speed.

The shortened days provide ample opportunity for reflection. Time is something we generally think we do not have enough of. The days go by too quickly and with each passing year they seem to become frenetically filled with more and more detail. It is commonly said that this is the inevitable result of the technological age. But is it? Living in the woods is allowing us to consider what is essential and what is not, and we are finding that life is calmer and more rewarding when lived with less clutter and stuff. If our home in Brome was equipped with so little as our cabin, we would be considered deprived. Yet here we miss none of the appliances and other add-ons.

We rejoice in the simplicity of our existence and relative lack of noise, particularly the intrusive, often untimely, ring of the phone. Yet we do not feel isolated by people being unable to

View from kitchen.

phone. Our family, our friends, and my clients know to send an e-mail if they want to talk to us. We then phone back. We only plug in the phone when we want to phone out, this to save from a drain on the solar system.

As noted previously, we have no running water, thus no taps. They might get in the way of the view. Here the dishwasher is me. There is no television. Radio-Canada, the only station we receive, albeit somewhat fuzzily, keeps us adequately informed. Living space is not a problem. A 54-square-metre (576-square-foot) cabin with a 25-square-metre (270-square-foot) loft is adequate for us, Scooter, and our guests. We want for nothing.

The chores become just things one does. Washing the dishes, chopping and fetching wood, cleaning the house, these all become simply activities. Do we wish there to come a day when we are less occupied? I think not. Being active is the key to life. It is the trivia which causes the time frustrations and we have been able to shed much of that.

Except for provisioning trips to La Tuque, Jeanne sticks strictly to her resolution to stay in the woods. She paints, keeps in touch with the children, grandchildren, and friends by e-mail, and produces her annual Christmas card. After supper, she is in her rocking chair, reading a book or doing a crossword puzzle, and, almost every night before going to bed, she does her yoga exercises in the loft.

I get up at 06:00 and relight the fires. Except on exceedingly cold nights when the temperature is −30°C (−22°F) or lower, we do not refuel during the night. On an average morning, the inside temperature will have fallen to circa 11°C (52°F). We keep both fires fueled until the inside temperature reaches 20°C (68°F). At that point, except on the very coldest of days, the cookstove will maintain that temperature. At cocktail time, we relight the heating stove and the temperature will rise to 23°C (73°F). Certain modifications were required to achieve this result.

The cabin is on posts and the wind blows off the frozen river, thereby chilling the floor. We think that Roch did not believe that we were really going to spend the winter here. Annually he hears members of the Club saying that they intend to visit in the winter. Few ever have. If Roch had known that we were serious, we think he would have more fully insulated the floor. To compensate, we have tacked tarpaulins around the perimeter of the underside of the cabin, banking them with snow. There are three doors to the cabin, two of which we have now sealed with plastic. The inside perimeter of the floor had been sealed with cement, but that disintegrated during the log-settling process and we have replaced it with wool insulation. We will caulk it in the spring. Jeanne continues to sew insulated curtains. She has a 1930 Singer Featherweight sewing machine which calls for less power than the new, modern, more fully equipped models. The large window overlooking the river she has already curtained. Come spring we should be ready for winter. The real concern is the speed with which we are consuming our wood supply. With the modifications, we have cut the consumption somewhat but not, I think, enough to see us through. I fell, block, and split yellow birch trees. We are mixing wet with dry wood in the stoves. Yellow birch burns wet!

After lighting the fires and visiting the outhouse, and while waiting for the coffee to filter, I write my daily diary entry. Without doing so, one day merges into the next and I fear that some of the

Oil painting, *Vermillion River*, by Jeanne Marler.

special moments would be forgotten. That done (Jeanne is still sleeping), I bring in firewood and start the generator to charge the solar batteries, which do not receive much sunlight at this time of year. If it has snowed, I climb onto the roof, safety rope installed, and sweep off the solar panels and satellite dish.

Jeanne spends the morning attending to her e-mails, the accounting of my law practice, housekeeping, and the preparation of the meals. Every so often the e-mails and office work are suspended and the easel appears. Her works of art will forever be a reminder of this year.

After lunch we embark on our daily snowshoe expeditions—and what a delight they are. Here, the snow does not come and go. It just comes. We are in classic cold-climate fluff. If it is windy, we generally stick to the portage trails along the river, which are in the woods. If it is calm, we head up the road which leads away from the cabin and examine the animal tracks. Now that the river is fully frozen, we can venture north to Lac de la Grande Baie, partially on the ice and partially on the portages. On that excursion there is a large marsh that is a joy to investigate. It is a moose

David, on Echo portage.

Jeanne, heading toward beaver lodge and dam. Photo David Marler.

David, hauling one bucket of water at a time in the winter.

yard area and frequented by many of our four-legged and winged winter friends.

Another modification has been the insulating of the hole in the river from which I draw the water. Initially I had a styrofoam panel sitting on the water. The water would freeze to its edges which required that I chop it free, inevitably leaving chunks of the material floating on the water. Then I realized that I could lay the sheet above, rather than in, the hole so that it would not touch the water, but it froze to the snow. I then conceived of laying two parallel planks under the styrofoam, and then covering it all with snow. This is most satisfactory. Now it is just a question of lifting the panel and chopping the ice. I normally take down four buckets. As the path down to the river is steep, I have run a rope banister between the trees. This means that only one bucket comes up at a time but this beats trying two, falling, and having to start again.

The evenings at this time of year come quickly enough and, with dinner and chat time, they are occupied by reading. Both Jeanne and I appreciate the reading suggestions we receive.

As I write, the days are supposedly getting longer. It's nice to know that we are now on the other side of the divide, but we are in no rush. This experience allows one to enjoy and cherish each day of the year without any desire that the seasons change more rapidly.

We knew, of course, that severely cold weather would arrive in due course. Our first dose of it commenced December 31, and continued through January 4, with overnight temperatures consistently in the low −30°C (−22°F) range, on January 2 hitting −40°, the temperature at which both Celsius and Fahrenheit meet.

Coping with the severe cold is a battle. Apart from trying to keep the inside temperature at an acceptably comfortable level (we regard that as being at 18°C [64°F]), outside activities are encumbered with problems. Fetching the water from the river means dealing with an immediate coat of ice forming on everything: the shovel, the axe, gloves, overalls, and boots. Fingers are constantly numb, particularly if one is trying to grip something. The pull-start of the chainsaw will not pull, and if it does, it will not recoil. The choke will not release. The chain is frozen to the bar.

One starts to think in survivalist terms. What if one has to "get out" and the snowmobile won't start? Most likely it will, on the pull-start, but what about the truck when we get to it? On any excursion into the woods beyond sight of the cabin, although this is routine in any weather, we are equipped with compass, flashlight, whistle (although there would be no one to hear it other than ourselves), knife, matches, snow goggles, and twine. On the snowmobile we always carry our snowshoes and an axe. The truck is equipped with a first aid kit, a saw to cut through trees which may have fallen on the road, sleeping bags and a tarpaulin in the event that we need to spend a night out in the cold, and a satellite phone.

Of course, one hopes never to have to use any of this emergency equipment. However, I am particularly concerned on the coldest nights when we are running both stoves at full tilt. What would we do if we had a fire in the middle of the night? What would be our procedure? I developed a plan and then asked Jeanne to describe hers. It was not at all the same as mine and we both realized that we would only compound an emergency situation by not being in sync.

The key to diminishing the risks is what Chris Hadfield, in his book *An Astronaut's Guide to Life on Earth*, calls SIMS, meaning simulated situations. And so guided by Commander Hadfield's book, we developed a SIMS. (1) One "warns" one's companions, (2) "gathers" them, and (3) "works" to implement the plan which has been discussed and practiced in simulated situations. We developed our plan and now sleep better at night. I recommend Commander Hadfield's book to everyone. One does not have to be a "space cadet" for it to have relevance. It would be especially beneficial to youngsters who are having difficulty in finding a career path. It is indeed a guide to living one's life.

December 14. The snow is starting to build up on the ground. It is time for me to take the truck to Le Relais; otherwise it will get snowed in at its parking place above the cabin. I loaded the snowmobile onto the back of the truck, using the loading ramp which Pierre Lemire had given me when I fetched the machine from him in the fall. Having unloaded the snowmobile at Le Relais, I cautiously returned on it to the cabin, this having been my first use of it and on snow which was only just deep enough to allow for its operation. All went well. Our routine for the rest of the winter will be to take the snowmobile to Le Relais, transfer to the truck, do what we have to do in La Tuque, return to Le Relais, transfer to the snowmobile and return to the cabin.

December 15. It is the Christmas concert day for the choir.

We went, as per the new routine, to Le Relais by snowmobile and then to La Tuque by truck. The concert was very special in that it showcased all three of the choirs of La Tuque: the children's choir, featuring some forty singers; us, La Brise du Nord; and Les Aînés, with some twenty voices. (The word *Aîné* means, literally, the first-born amongst siblings, hence the eldest. Thus a group of such could, at a stretch, be called "the elders"—or "Les Aînés.") The magnificent church in which we sang, L'Église Saint-Zéphirin, was full. It seats upwards of 350 persons in the pews. After the concert was the Christmas supper for the members of the La Brise du Nord, held at Le Club de Golf of La Tuque. The supper was a great success as it afforded Jeanne and me the opportunity to talk in a social context, really for the first time, to people from La Tuque. Choir practices are not, after all, opportunities for conversation, unless one wishes to court a rebuke from the choir director. We were invited to sit at the table of the mayor, M. Normand Beaudoin and his wife, Mme Kathleen Bonenfant, who had introduced me to the choir, as previously mentioned.

The 411 was in good shape though the snow was falling heavily, which hindered our vision but, we thought, would improve our return to the cabin on the snowmobile from Le Relais.

We switched over to the snowmobile at Le Relais. The snow on Clubhouse Road had been packed as a result of the previous passage of snowmobiles. However, when turning off to take "our road" down to the cabin, my vision was suddenly obscured by snow, illuminated by the machine's headlight, flying up onto the windshield. That, I subsequently realized, may happen if one leaves a packed trail, as we had just done, to take an untracked trail with fresh, fluffy snow on it. As a result, I could not see the direction of the trail and we ended up capsizing into a ditch. We were deposited on our backs with our legs partially under the overturned machine. We assessed our situation from our inverted, side-by-side positions, decided that neither of us was hurt, and turned our attention to trying to get our legs out from under the machine. By wiggling our feet and legs, we were able to extract one leg each. We then applied our freed feet to the seat of the snowmobile and began to rock it. Bit by bit we extracted our other legs. Nothing much we could do at that point other than snowshoe the rest of the way. Yes, we had remembered to take snowshoes with us, in case of precisely this type of situation. I was, of course upset (no pun intended) by what had just occurred, but before long the pleasure of snowshoeing on a temperate and snowy night was therapeutic.

The next morning, I packed up my rope and my come-along and was about to head out the door to snowshoe back to the machine when I heard the sound of a snowmobile. Moments later a man was at our door. He was Guy Roy, a person we had been told about, a trapper with a cabin some fifteen kilometres (eight miles) from us. He had been out checking his trap lines and had, as our good fortune would have it, taken the track in our direction from the turnoff above Le Relais. He had seen the overturned snowmobile in the ditch. He then followed our snowshoe tracks to us. I told him what I was about to do and what equipment I had prepared to extract the machine. He said I would not need my equipment and invited me to embark behind him on his machine, and off we went. Upon arriving at the scene, he took from his equipment box a length of strapping which, in these parts, is called *un bender* (why, I am not sure), which he attached to the rear of his machine and then to mine. We righted my machine and I started its motor. He told me not to try to drive out of the ditch but to apply minimal throttle, just so that the track would turn, once his machine was pulling. He remounted his machine and slowly but surely extracted mine. Upon departing, he said he would come back to visit us at some point to see how we were getting along. I thanked him profusely. He refused to accept any compensation.

This is not the last you will hear of Guy. He made a point, in that first winter, of dropping by from time to time to check up on us and answer our questions. He became one of our mentors.

In his book *A Guide to Nature in Winter*, Donald Stokes writes: "*More than just an impression in the snow, a trail is like a rope connecting*

disparate moments in time, both a record of the past and a connection to the present, for back on the trail are sketched the encounters of a living being, while ahead is the present animal leaving its life experience one step behind."

We find an abundance of tracks of the snowshoe hare and regularly the evidence of a scary and sometimes fateful encounter, e.g., the imprint in the snow of the wing of the owl that descended silently upon the hare. We have also encountered the entrails of a hare, all that was left from the moment of its demise. Partridges are in abundance. While they generally roost in trees, on very cold nights they will dive into the snow to spend a night in an instant insulated chalet. One will also see, from their wing imprints in the snow, the place where they exploded the next morning from their burrow to roost again in the trees.

On one of our snowshoe excursions, we saw what appeared at first glance to be an impossibly large red squirrel in the higher branches of a yellow birch. It was a marten. This taught us to scan the tree tops. By doing so, one improves one's chances of seeing a porcupine and in the spring a bear or, more likely, bear cubs.

Oil painting, *Partridge,* by Jeanne Marler

Mink are often seen along the shore of the river. In the fall, we observed a solitary Canada goose in the bay. The next morning the bay was littered with goose tail and wing feathers. No sign of the goose. Maybe it got away, but the site of the battle was undoubtedly the occasion of an encounter with a mink. A similar occurrence was a summer night which erupted in the racket of a contest of some sort on the shore. In the morning, we found the feathers of a night heron. The mink strikes again?

From the tracks themselves it is often difficult to determine exactly what animal passed by, but there are other clues. If the animal has urinated and if one kneels down and sniffs, one will know whether it was of the canine or feline family. The canines in these parts are fox and wolf; if a feline, almost certainly a lynx. The mink, as another clue, leaves its poop on the top of small rocks. Thus, the daily snowshoe is not just exercise. It is a fascinating exploration of the lives of our neighbours, the animals of the territory.

Many have asked: What about bears? Of course, during the winter they are in hibernation. In the other seasons bears are rarely seen, since this is not an area populated by humans leaving their waste exposed, although scat is regularly found on the trails. We do not feed the birds in the winter for the reason that the seeds with which we would feed them would become a lure for the bears in the spring.

Moose are often seen and one cannot miss their prints or their having gnawed on the smaller branches of the poplars and birches. We found an overnight bed in the snow not 200 metres (circa 200 yards) from the cabin. Wolf tracks are also prevalent on our road.

I was constantly mindful that we were quickly running out of wood. This led to thoughts of how to reduce its consumption. The improvements to be addressed would include adding insulation to the floor of the cabin, sealing any air-entry points, particularly around the interior perimeter of the cabin floor, and correcting

Bull Moose.

Moose markings on sapling.

the condensation buildup on the ceiling, which necessitated the strategic placing in the loft of buckets to catch the drips, with plastic sheets over anything that had to be kept dry.

I researched this problem and learned that the condensation problem occurs in cold climates when the interior temperature of a building is considerably higher than the exterior temperature—precisely our situation—and where there is no vapor barrier and/or adequate ventilation in the roof. This was

These are all moose tracks.

not a problem that could be dealt with before the late spring or summer. It would require an extensive renovation of the roof. The root of the problem resulted, as I have previously mentioned, from Roch not having believed that we would spend the winter in the cabin. However, if we could get an airtight stove to the cabin in the middle of the winter we would, at least, reduce to some degree the consumption of the firewood and eliminate the need to refuel in the middle of the night.

On February 26 I set off for Trois-Rivières ("Three-Rivers"), where I had found a stove dealer. It was a snowy day, which meant that I would have the unnerving experience, and not for the first time, of being blinded by dense clouds of swirling snow every time I would pass a lumber truck coming from the opposite direction. But in due course I made it. An hour or so later, a beautiful, airtight, sandstone stove was loaded onto the back of the truck. It was choir practice night, so I stayed in La Tuque. Jeanne, I learned the next morning, needed to get up twice during the night to refuel the soon-to-be-replaced stove.

I had arranged with Roch and Paul to meet me at Le Relais, and, with the help of another person who was there, we successfully manhandled the stove out of the truck and semi-lifted, semi-dropped it into the sled of Roch's snowmobile. Then the fifteen-minute snowmobile run to the cabin, and an hour or so later the new stove was installed and operational. The stove holds its fire for up to nine hours, and most mornings I did not need to relight, just refuel. What a relief, and what a difference that made to our lives. Certainly, the insulation problems would need to be resolved but they would have to await the summer. Meanwhile, the rapid diminution of our wood supply continued, albeit less quickly. However, a saviour was to appear.

Over our many years at the Club we had come to meet members of the Fecteau family. They have a camp on Lac Elie, some three kilometres (two miles) from the Club and approximately the same distance from our cabin. One day in early March, we heard the sound of approaching snowmobiles. Our visitors were Marc Fecteau and his friend Richard Crête, who were on a snowmobile excursion to see if we were "at home." I had seen

Empty woodshed.

them during moose-hunting season and had invited them to visit us, not that they needed an invitation. Upon their arrival, Marc noticed our very diminished pile of wood in the woodshed. He offered to let me raid their supply. Had this chance encounter not occurred I am not sure what we would have done. But once again we were being looked after. Over the course of the next few days I took loads of my freshly cut *merisier* up to the Fecteau camp and exchanged them for loads of dry wood sufficient to see us through. *Merci mille fois, Marc.*

6

Spring 2014

Something's happening. It started in late February. The winter song of the chickadee is fading and being replaced by its summer sound. Birds are coming around the cabin, including a chickadee that sits on Jeanne's shoulder. They no longer need the protection of the deep woods. It is not the temperature that accounts for this but rather the lengthening days that causes them to sense the arrival of spring. As late as the third week of March we were still experiencing lows down to −33°C (−27°F). With the arrival of March, we started to have real winter snowstorms. We had had none of significance until then. We certainly had lots of snow on the ground. It had come down in quantities of one to four centimetres (an inch or two). Now it is coming down in dig-out quantities. The winds have strengthened and are pushing the snow into waist-high drifts, making us bundle up and keep the fires going.

And then it happened—on March 18, to be precise—the arrival of the first of those classic March days. The day started at −30°C (−22°F) but by noon was up to +4°C (39°F) under a strong sun, cloudless sky, and no wind. We had an early lunch and then packed our knapsacks for an excursion, the knapsacks needed because we knew we would be shedding clothing. We went east up the old logging road which we use to get to our camp, north

David, March snowshoe.

Jeanne. Photo David Marler.

into Moose Swamp, then to Moose Lake. Then we continued up onto the old logging road that runs parallel to ours, and gazed south over the valley of the invisible river below us, while a three-toed woodpecker hammered away on a dead *merisier*.

We then went west, following the road for a while, and bushwhacked the last 500 metres (circa 500 yards) in very deep snow to the river. We stopped for a rest and then plodded over the snow-drifted frozen river back to camp. I say "plodded" because water on top of the ice froze on the snowshoes, which made the end of our excursion somewhat tedious.

Later that week, our crew of woodcutters arrived: Roch; Paul; Roch's son, Pierre; and Pierre's wife, Anick. Two days later, fifteen cords of split wood lay piled in a mound waiting for me to stack it in the woodshed.

Stacking firewood is a long but very satisfying job. It takes a few weeks if one is doing it alone, but it is a fine activity for April and early May. Our daily snowshoe excursions gradually ceased as the quality of the snow decreased. Snowshoeing in slushy snow is a drag, and walks are really not that pleasant as they eventually become mud walks. So it is the time to stack wood and listen to the birds, absorb the arrival of spring, and for Jeanne to paint.

The river stays frozen until the second week of May, on average. This year may set a record late ice-out date, given the exceptional cold of the winter and depth of the ice. The snowdrifts on the lake are helping my hole in the ice, snow being a superb insulator. Soon the ice will start receding from the shores. Fetching the water at that point will become a wet experience because of the slush on top of the ice.

The warmth of the sun is more evident every day and the woods are alive with activity.

March 21. I picked up my eighty-three-year-old cousin, Alan French, at the Montreal bus station, his home being in Andover, Massachusetts. At 19:00 we were at La Tuque and at Le Relais by 20:30.

The drive on the 411 was not easy. I admired the calm and fortitude with which Alan endured the swings and slides through the snow and ice on the 411 and, even more so, on the snowmobile ride in the dark to the cabin. Our road was badly drifted, requiring me to constantly shift my weight to keep the snowmobile upright. I was successful until I arrived almost at the door to our cabin, where I encountered the biggest drift, which had been

Alan French.

caused by the wind coming off the river. Alan was unceremoniously discharged from the snowmobile as it rolled onto its side,
but with no harm done.

Alan is an enthusiastic outdoors person and loves to stack
wood! Our days together at the cabin resulted in nearly all the
wood being stacked into the woodshed. All that remained were
the logs buried and frozen in the snow on the ground. Our evenings were a series of discussions, punctuated by Alan playing his
harmonica, me singing along.

After a winter of just Jeanne and me, with the exception of
occasional daytime visits, it was a lift to have another energy in
the cabin. On the evening of the last day of his visit, we celebrated
with moose stew, the cut of meat coming courtesy of our friends
from Lac-Édouard, Véronique and Denis. (See Jeanne's recipe for
moose stew in the "Recipes" section.)

❧

March 25. Overnight exterior temperature: −26°C [−8°F]. Daytime high 15°C [59°F].

Navigating the 411 in the winter is nearly always an adventure, something which I accepted as a challenge but which Jeanne endured with white knuckles. We had been to Brome to ready the house for our new tenants from France, Luc and Sylvie Robert. On our return trip, the 411 was completely thawed in places, which meant, in some places, dredging the truck through muck and slush. When driving through shaded areas, we contended with slabs of ice 7.4 centimetres (3 inches) thick. Once at Le Relais we transferred everything, as usual, from the truck to the snowmobile sled and off we went, again experiencing diminishing snow conditions. Of course, yet again we got stuck by wandering, though only marginally, off the packed trail and into deep, wet, and rotting snow. We snowshoed the last two kilometres (1.3 miles) carrying our purchases, making two further trips to bring it all to the camp. And then back again, to free the snowmobile, with my trusty come-along, rope, and other paraphernalia.

April 9. We made another trip to Brome. While we were away, Paul had been *chez nous*, cat-sitting and attending to our never-ending list of things that needed to be done. Upon our return at 16:30, he left by snowmobile for his home in La Tuque.

I was concerned that he would be on the trail alone, a run of seventy-four kilometres (fifty miles). There would likely be no other snowmobilers on the trail, given that it was the middle of the week and that the snowmobiling season was over. Paul said, "*Pas de problème*," and who was I to argue with a seasoned man of the great outdoors.

April 10. It had been a warm night with outside temperature at 06:00 being −6°C [21°F]. At noon, there was a knock at the door. A hooded man, seemingly ill, was leaning against the doorframe.

It was Paul! His snowmobile had broken down the previous evening some eleven kilometres (seven miles) from Le Relais. Paul thought he might be able to find a cabin where he could sleep, but after a couple of hours without success he returned to the snowmobile, detached the sled, found a sheltered spot under fir trees, turned the sled over, crawled under it and spent the night there. He had his sleeping bag with him as well as some food. In the morning he walked back to us, a distance of fifteen kilometres (ten miles). He plunked himself down in my big recliner chair and fell asleep. He refused to get into our guest bed in the loft. He was sore, tired, a little hungry, and very thirsty. We could not reach Roch. Perhaps he and his wife, Alma, were in Cuba, a place much visited by the people of La Tuque. April is a good time to go south from this climate.

Jeanne and I presumed that Paul would spend the night with us and that in the morning I would drive him to La Tuque. He could then return with whatever and whomever he needed to retrieve his snowmobile. But no, at 15:00 he wanted to leave and get home. His plan was that we would ride my snowmobile to his and tow it back to Le Relais. I would then drive him in the truck to his home in La Tuque and he would retrieve his snowmobile from Le Relais in due course. And so it worked out, and once again I was the recipient of an education from teacher Paul, particularly in how to harness a snowmobile to be towed by another; not to its skis but to the arms that attach the skis to the frame of the machine. One removes the drive belt from the machine to be towed. Easier said than done, but in due course accomplished, and eventually we were back at Le Relais, into the truck and out onto the 411. It was in the worst condition that I had seen it, and I can say that I have never since seen it as bad. I needed to put the truck into locked four-wheel drive on more than one occasion, and we slowly ground our way through the slush, snow, ice, and mud and eventually arrived at his home. He wanted to pay me for the gas. I refused and told him that it was I who was indebted to him due to all of the things that I was learning from him.

It just so happened that it was choir practice night. As usual, I stayed overnight in La Tuque. In any event, I would not have wanted to tackle the 411 again on that same day. In the morning, I left to return home to the cabin, wondering in what condition I would find the road. The temperature was −10°C and the road had refrozen. It was a rough ride but without any problem or excitement.

Spring washout on our road.

April 12. Scooter has emerged from her deep winter hibernation. She slept the winter away, waking only to eat. Now she is outside all night. While she can now go everywhere she wants, we have become very restricted. Our road and what was the snowmobile track hold only intermittent patches of snow. Major culverts are still frozen such that the streams are passing over the surface of the road.

April 13. Any trip to La Tuque would involve the 5-km [3-mile] walk to Le Relais and back. It is also practically impossible to move about outside. The snow is too soft and slushy for either snowshoes or walking. There is still almost a metre [more than two feet] of snow covering the ground. Thus, all outside activity is restricted unless a cold night puts a crust on the snow. Then early morning snowshoeing is exceedingly rewarding, as one can literally go anywhere. But stay out too long and one will be dragging oneself out of wet, clinging snow-holes. We knew that this period would come at some point at about this time of year, and we are stocked for at least three weeks. As the snow recedes, many logs are appearing from under the snow and waiting to be split and to be stacked in the woodshed. It is also the ideal time to burn the slash from trees downed by the winter storms. The river channel has opened, as have areas over shallows and rocks. Fetching water from the river is a wet and slippery task.

April 15. 1°C [34°F] at 06:00. 17°C [63°F] at 15:00. Cocktails on the porch for the first time since the fall and a declaration that "winter is over." The ground is still covered in snow but the air is warm, mornings invariably dawning with fog on the river and frozen crystals on the trees.

❧

Condensation in rapids.

Rob Paterson wanted me to write an article for his *Tempo* blog about our outhouse. What exactly he wanted to know and why, I was not inclined to ask. So I just gave him my take on the structure. Here's what I wrote for his blog:

First, you will note from the photograph that it was constructed in the same architectural style as the cabin—which is, I think,

Outhouse.

aesthetically pleasing. Second, its physical location is important: it is downwind of the cabin (prevailing wind is from the west) and situated just beyond the woodshed, which allows one to bring in an armful of wood from the woodshed upon one's return from the outhouse. This latter point—the outhouse's situation in respect to the prevailing wind—needs no explanation. In Calvin Rutstrum's *The Wilderness Cabin* (1961) (a book which Jeanne gave me on the occasion of our third wedding anniversary to celebrate laying the foundation of the log cabin at Lac Tremblant in the late sixties), Rutstrum writes: "In today's world, the outside toilet is mentioned only in shocked whispers. With rare exceptions, almost every one of these structures is unpleasant. And yet the outside toilet can be . . . inoffensive." He then describes the essentials, which I will paraphrase:

Make sure the toilet seat has a cover and that the cover fits snuggly over the seat. When not in use, lower the cover. Cross-ventilate the pit by making the sides air-penetrable. All ventilation gaps should be screened to prevent the entry of mosquitoes and the like. Install a vertical pipe to act as a ventilation channel from the pit up to and through the roof of the structure. Allow for screened cross-ventilation under the roof.

This method of building an outhouse is subject to variation, but it is to say that not all outhouses need to be offensive and ours is not—or, at least, I hope that Rob did not think so when he visited. We keep a container of ashes in the outhouse. We do not lack for ashes, given that we heat and cook using wood-burning stoves. There is a scooper to drop the ashes into the hole. Every two or three days I shovel out the hole and transfer the contents into a pit some distance away, and I regularly cover the pit with ashes. A friend has asked: "But how do you shovel out the hole?" The answer, which I only discovered once Roch and Paul had finished the construction of our outhouse, is to build it at the top of a slope, the door on the upper side, leaving the back, on the slope behind, open. Thus, it is from outside and behind the construction that one can, with a long-handled shovel, reach the pit and shovel it out.

What is important, at least to us, is the essential purity of the institution. It requires no plumbing, no septic tank, and no weeping field. It uses no water. It does not back up, and thus does not require a plunger; it demands no cleansing products, which are almost necessarily toxic, to shine its nonexistent porcelain.

On one of my recent visits to Brome, a reader remarked, "You are living just as my grandparents did on the farm." It was said with an air of nostalgia. For many, in days gone by but still within living memory, the outhouse was the norm. Rural folk used outhouses and suffered no embarrassment in so doing. Society has now gone to the extreme of considering that there should be almost as many bathrooms in a house as there are bedrooms, preferably "*en suite.*"

The choice of living in a 7.5 × 7.5 metre (24 × 24 foot), one-and-a-half-floor dwelling without running water eliminates the time, effort, and expense of the nonessentials—and with no loss of comfort. It is this simplification that makes living in the woods so enjoyable. I am not suggesting that everyone should ditch the flush toilet and build an outhouse. Indeed, in non-rural areas such would be socially unacceptable and likely illegal.

And consider this: how often does one get outside on a clear night to relish the brilliance of the stars and of the northern lights?

We have witnessed this magical phenomenon, an extravaganza of various coloured streams of light seeking to penetrate the heavens, in a variety of places: Jeanne and I both saw the "lights" at Lac Tremblant; Jeanne saw them while on a group excursion to James Bay in the Canadian Arctic; I saw them once in Brome; and, of course, we saw them at our cabin. However, the sighting of the lights is rare for the reason that one is so rarely outside at night, and to have the chance to see the "lights," one has to be in a place with relatively unrestricted views of the sky, and this was not the case for us at our cabin. Our view to the north is restricted by heavily wooded, rising land. That is not to say that we did not see the lights on occasion, but, because of the trees, the experience could not be as dramatic as it might have been.

When spring eventually arrived, it came with a rush. The activity in nature was frenetic. At this latitude it is even more frenetic than it is in more temperate regions. The time is shorter. The breeding must begin at once if there is to be time for the newborns to be ready to migrate or survive the coming cold of the next Canadian winter.

Our first sighting of the Canada geese was on April 26. Gulls and mergansers were on the river on April 27. On April 28, we heard but did not see a loon. One appeared on the river the following day and the other arrived on May 3, and that was a cause for celebration at cocktail hour on the porch, although we were still dressed in winter clothes, with hats and gloves. This was the figurative end of Jeanne's "Year," the year having been defined by the migration of the loons.

And thus, the originally conceived year in the woods came to its end, but we felt that we were still just settling in. To go back to civilization at this point would have been to abandon a project which we had only just begun, leaving before we had completed what needed to be done in order to leave the cabin in a truly finished state and, perhaps most importantly, before we had had the opportunity to fully savour the experience of living in this remote setting. However, that was all academic for the time being, given that our home back in Brome was rented until April 2015. We would now have time to complete the cabin by attending to the improvements that would advance it from being a qua-si-primitive shelter to an abode of wilderness perfection. There was yet much to be done.

Here is what I wrote for *Tempo* that spring:

The merry month of May is here! The woods are full of move-ment. On May 3 Jeanne saw a fox stalking a hare. I saw a lynx on the 411. The winter wren sings for us every morning. The daily parade of the skeins of geese is constant and will continue well into early June.

Snow-free patches are starting to appear. Moving about remains difficult. However, by now I am able to tackle the spring cleanup, remove the tarpaulins from around the perimeter of the cabin, bring the canoes out from under it, replace the styrofoam seat on the toilet with the wooden one, repair the windbreak protecting the vegetable garden, tidy up the decks, split the last of the logs that had been buried under the snow, and plan for the insulation of the floor, a project which will, no doubt, consume me daily for the entire summer and fall, with a better result, I hope, than my failed project of last summer and fall of attempting to build a cold cellar.

The cold cellar (sometimes called a root cellar) project was a time-consuming and, ultimately, futile exercise. In our early contemplations of our life in the woods, we thought it only appropriate that we should have a cold cellar. It was, after all, a standard feature of homesteads and country living before the advent of electricity, and we have one, which I constructed, in the basement of our home in Brome. The beauty of living in the country is that one can store quantities of fresh vegetables and fruit, grown in the garden and on the property, in the cold cellar, as opposed to being restricted to the limited space of a refrigerator and freezer, and having to go to the market every week to purchase food. As with so many things in the postindustrial world, society leapt at the new technological inventions, of which the greatest, perhaps, were the automobile and electricity. It all became so easy. One just drove to the supermarket. One did not have to have a provisioning plan to last a month or so. One just went shopping. If one forgot something, one just went back for it.

However, there is always a price to be paid, which includes the purchase cost of the gasoline and, not to be forgotten, the environmental costs. Moreover, nothing in a store can be as fresh as home-grown food, and yet the vast mass of North Americans adhere to the so-called conveniences. Certainly, purchasing store-bought food is less expensive than buying at specialty organic-food outlets, but what are our priorities? Do we, as a community, rank convenience over health? I am afraid that the answer is yes—and what is the cost of that? Given all these considerations, it was simply part of our lives to have a cold cellar—plus the fact that shopping for us, from our cabin in the woods, entailed a considerable expedition.

So, as soon as the ground had unfrozen in the spring of our first year, I started to dig. Once I had removed the accumulation of rotted balsam needles, leaves, and wood at the site I had chosen, I encountered rock. With my shovel and heavy metal bar I chipped away at it and, with great difficulty and perseverance, I found ways to remove the rocks from this side or that—which, unfortunately, encouraged me to continue. The spring passed by and the hole became deeper. The summer passed by and the hole became wider. The fall came and I was still at it, to the point where it was now about four feet deep, and that was deep enough. I had calculated the number of board feet of hemlock I would need to build the structure. I went into La Tuque, bought the lumber, brought it back in my truck and its trailer, carried it all by hand down to the cellar site from the parking area, and started to construct.

In the construction, I was greatly aided by Robert Poupart, a friend from the Eastern Townships, who is much more experienced in construction than I. He took over the direction of the project and there emerged a magnificent cold cellar, with antechamber and double doors.

David and Robert Poupart discussing root cellar design.

It was then or shortly thereafter, as I was installing the air vents and inserting the shelves upon which the produce would be stored, that we came into a period of three days of continuous rain, and water accumulated to a depth of about thirty centimetres (one foot) in the bottom of my cellar. I borrowed a gasoline pump from Roch and pumped the water out. The next day I went to inspect. The water was right back up to the same level. I pumped it out again . . . and the next day it was there again. There was no apparent entry point for the water to get into the cellar. It was just there. I decided that the solution was to dig into the cellar from the outside on its lower side so that the water could flow out. The problem was that, in making the cellar, I had already dug down as far as one could go, which meant that I could not create an exit for the water at a lower level than where I had already reached. I had discovered the Laurentian Shield. It was no longer merely something I had learned about, with limited attention, in school. Now it was the real thing and, in any event, this layer of solid rock probably has a limited capacity to store residual heat in the winter or residual cold in the summer. It is the capacity of the ground to store heat and cold that makes a cold cellar work.

Once again, Roch and Paul, who had witnessed this exercise intermittently on their visits to us, were discreet. I had to find out for myself and, in hindsight, I am happy that I did, because it was just another part of learning about where we had chosen to live. I finally dismantled my cold cellar and in so doing accumulated a pile of hemlock boards, for what future use I do not know, and I retrieved the hundreds of screws which had gone into the cellar's construction. So not all was lost and my education of living in the north increased.

Cabin without the root cellar.

May 8. We will, in a week or so, be able to return the truck from Le Relais to its parking spot above the cabin. However, we must wait for Clubhouse Road to thaw completely, for otherwise any use of it would result in its being damaged. Overnight temperatures are still below zero [32°F].

I was always a little concerned about leaving the truck at Le Relais. In the winter I was less concerned, for generally the staff of Le Relais were present. However now, with the 411 being passable and Le Relais closed, well, one never knows.

May 9. Roch and Paul visited on their way to the Clubhouse, their first possible visit of the season. They plan to redo the cabin roof in July. Since they were using Clubhouse Road, it was time for us to fetch the truck. We walked out to Le Relais and drove the truck back, with the loading/unloading ramp for the skidoo in the back, to its parking spot above the cabin.

We store the snowmobile on the ramp covered by a Tempo, one of those tent-like structures which people use as garages in the winter, and which we had recently bought on a trip to La Tuque. Our requirement, however, was not for the winter but the other three seasons when the snowmobile is not used. Keeping the sun off the machine is important, as eventually, if it is not covered, the rubberized parts of it would decay.

It was a spectacularly beautiful day, with a high of 11°C (52°F). After supper, we each took a glass of wine down to the bench which I had made and installed on the riverbank above the shore. We watched the loons floating on the glassy surface of the river and then saw something causing a significant wake and swimming down the river, obligingly in our direction. It was a very large beaver. It seemed to be investigating the shore for a good place to make a future lodge. There used to be beavers close to our cabin site, as evidenced by old stumps of trees that had been felled and then carted off by these enterprising creatures. However, our shore, as earlier recounted, is wide open to the westerly wind and would not, we thought, be a good spot for our furry and tooth-equipped visitor to build. He moved on, and where he eventually built his lodge, we do not know.

May 10. Fishing season is open. In fact, it has been officially open since the last week of April, but the river, until today, was still covered in ice.

I knew it was too early to expect a catch but nonetheless thought that I might give it a try. In the late afternoon, I walked over to the rapids and limbered up my casting. The river was in spate—fast and swollen with the spring runoff. I normally wade right in to it to avoid catching my backcasts on the tree-lined shore, but not in this condition of current—I would have been swept away. As predicted, no bites.

May 11. Saw yellow-rumped and black-poll warblers and a black-backed woodpecker. Later in the day a great horned owl passed by over the shore, and later still a great blue heron winged its way from the rapids of the river, where it fishes, to its home in Chaloupe Bay.

Chaloupe Bay is along the northern shore of the river and is so called because a *chaloupe* (small motorboat) resides there permanently but is used only once a year, in the spring, to fish below the Echo Rapids, those being the rapids we look at directly to the west of the cabin. The owner of the *chaloupe* is a "wormer," and he hauls his limit out of that fertile and productive spot without any difficulty. But that is only once a year. Thus, I am not concerned. Nor am I concerned that he will ever broadcast his secret location. He no more wants other people to learn of the spot than we do, the members of the Club.

View from large western facing windows, looking at the rapids.

May 14. I went out to go to Montreal on business. The 411 was free of snow but not free of water flowing from the streams where the culverts were still frozen. One very impressive but not quite total washout of the road was caused by beavers.

May 15. High of 25°C [77°F]. Black flies are out. On the birding front: winter wren, hummingbird, song sparrow, Swainson's thrush. Loons did a mating dance on the river. It lasted about half an hour. It consisted of high-speed bursts of running along the surface of the water, vigorous wing flapping, and then diving.

May 16. Our friends Danny Braün and Seana Pašić arrived from Montreal. They are enthralled by our situation. Danny, who knows the woods from his childhood, expressed a keen desire to one day do what we are doing. We love it when they visit whether here or at home in

Seana Pašić and Danny Braün.

Brome. Danny loves to cook. When they are staying with us, Jeanne gets a break from the kitchen.

Tonight was *magret de canard* with the trimmings, with pear/ginger upside-down cake for dessert, accompanied by an appropriate assortment of wines. Danny and Seana stayed for a week. We ate very well and worked it off by making various excursions. In addition, Danny is an enthusiastic log-splitter and stacker. It was fun to have company in my daily activity. Seana is an unofficially adopted daughter, a refugee from the Balkan wars, and kindred spirit of Jeanne's.

May 17. First full immersion swim in the lake.

I used to celebrate the Queen's birthday ("Patriots' Day" in Quebec) every year on May 24 with a ducking in the river. Danny and Seana's enthusiasm upped the ante and advanced the date. Jeanne acted as photographer of the record-breaking event. The photograph has been censored.

May 19. A trip to La Tuque to sing with the choir at the funeral of André Drolet, a much-loved member of the choir and the La Tuque community. The choir sang Gregory Charles's evocative and beautiful composition: "*Sous d'autres cieux*" (literally: "under other skies").

May 24. The yearling moose are moving about, having been told by their parents to "go find your own home."

This means that we sometimes see moose swimming across the river in front of the cabin. It always means sightings on the forestry roads. They are such gangly critters at that age, their developing bodies on top of long, spindly legs.

May 25. Monsieur Chaloupe is fishing at Echo Rapids. Jeanne planted peas in our garden, taking refuge in the cabin from time to time to escape the black flies. On our daily walk, we saw a hare nibbling on the new shoots beside the track, quite unconcerned by our presence.

May 26. Started building another above-ground garden bed, this one sheltered from the wind by the cabin. Before adding imported soil and compost, I raked scraps of wood from in front of the woodshed, the result of March's splitting spree. However, I quickly came down to a solidly frozen layer of ice. I needed to re-cover it with the scraps I had raked up, otherwise we would have had a dangerously slippery path to the outhouse.

SNOWSHOE HARE

Slow

Fast

Hind feet in front

May 28. Down to the river with rod.

There comes a time every year in the spring when that pool I love to fish becomes frenetically alive. As the fly flashes through the water, pulled downstream by the fast current, the speckled trout will jump right out of the water in their excitement. On one of my first casts, a hit. In that water, one often thinks one has a monster on the line but more often it is the force of the current than the size of the fish which causes one to think that. The little ones quickly tire of the fight, and I slip them off my barbless

A fish worth keeping!

hook and return them to the river. But today I landed a fish worthy of keeping for a meal. One of the great treats of life is to have the privilege of eating a grilled, freshly caught speckled trout.

May 30. Started to lug down from the parking area 40 bags of soil and compost.

May 31. Jeanne Talbot, a friend from our Senneville days, and her beau, Earl Atnikov, arrived today, and by late afternoon the remaining 36 bags of soil and compost were brought down and stacked, ready to be emptied on the bed.

Even more remarkable, from a timing point of view, Nathalie Bergeron had been to Montreal to pick up the tomato plants she had ordered, along with ours. She gave ours to her husband Richard, who gave them to Jeanne and Earl when they registered at *la barrière*. What timing!

June 2. A warm overcast day, ideal weather for the mosquitoes, which are out in force and in the cabin.

When we're inside during the day, mosquitoes are not too much of a menace because they are easy to swat. However, at night when one is in bed, their presence, announced by their buzzing, is mental torture. One does not want to turn on the light to try to see them: one is trying to go to sleep. One swats where one thinks they are, normally one's head around the ears,

Making the vegetable garden with Jeanne Talbot and Earl
Atnikov, May, 2014.

for it is the ear that tells one they are there—but the buzzing soon returns.

Jeanne, amongst her many talents, is a student of natural remedies and in particular aromatherapy, which means (excuse me if you already know, but I had to look it up in the dictionary): "the use of aromatic plant extracts and essential oils for therapeutic purposes." Thus, any complaint in her household is treated with an essential oil from her box containing dozens of little bottles, each containing the remedy to be applied, whether ingested or wiped onto the troubled area.

The recipe for mosquitoes is to combine the following essential oils: four drops each of thyme, lavender, and peppermint, and eight drops of lemongrass (cf. *The Fragrant Pharmacy* by Valerie Ann Worwood). Put two drops of the mix on a cotton wool ball on your bedside table. Jeanne puts one on her side of the bed and one on mine. No more random desperate spraying of toxic repellants which, if effective at all, are only so for a minute or two. On our walks in the woods, Jeanne stuffs two swabs moistened with her mixture under her cap. (See "Jeanne's Essential Oils 'Pharmacy,'" following the "Recipes" section in the back of the book.)

June 3. A sunny day with high cover of thin cloud. At about 16:30 I again had a feeling that it was a fishing day. I was right. A keeper at over one kilogram (2.5 pounds). It made for a fine and much appreciated supper. There are many ways to cook trout, of course, but my favourite is always the simplest, to wit: the frying pan in butter.

A late skein of geese flew over. I thought at the time that this must be the last of this year's migration. It does not matter, at least not to me, how many skeins I hear. I cannot avoid looking up when I hear them. In separate skeins are the snow geese. In the early morning when the sunshine reflects on the underside of their wings, it is as if one is watching an electric light show.

June 5. Built a stockade wall to protect the vegetable garden from the prevailing westerlies coming off the river.

I cut four balsam poles, 7.5 centimetres (three inches) in diameter by about four metres (twelve feet) long, and dug them into the ground (easier said than done) 7.5 centimeters (three inches) apart, two at each end of my planned wall. I then cut the necessary number of poles and slotted them in horizontally between the uprights. This effort notwithstanding, weeks later we realized that although that location was the one with the maximum daily period of exposure to the sun, we could not completely eliminate the effect of the wind. The poor plants just would not grow. So, as described earlier, we expanded the garden in the lee of the cabin, and there we had great success with tomatoes, basil, garlic, pole beans, parsley, and roquette lettuce.

Paul Bérubé came down from the Clubhouse to adjust the doors, windows and screens of the cabin. You will recall that I discussed the shrinking of the logs which occurs with unseasoned wood for at least two years after their installation. Nothing had broken. The doors and windows had simply become difficult to open and shut. We were thankful that Paul took the time from his duties at the Clubhouse to come to us. This is the time of year when the members of the Club appear in force, for the first two weeks of June are the optimum fishing time. Sometimes there is great success, sometimes nothing or close to nothing. That is the intrigue of fishing. Any disappointment is rapidly alleviated, once the members are back at the Clubhouse, by the telling of the tales of previous successes and adventures, stoked with the nectar which brings forth and exaggerates the memories.

This year's episode involved two members getting a dunking in the river. The landings at the head of rapids, particularly on rivers once used for the annual spring log drives, were built very close to the beginning of the rush of the water in order to make the carries over the portages as short as possible. The only safe way for canoeists to approach such a landing when going downstream is to turn the canoe 180 degrees at the landing so that it faces upriver, which allows one to retain control. This manoeuvre involves the bow person employing his/her paddle as a brake, called a bow rudder. To put this another way, to approach a landing by heading downstream can result in disaster if one misses.

In this particular case, the disaster was not, fortunately, to the two intrepid fishermen who, although dumped unceremoniously into the water, were able to scramble ashore. The canoe, however, continued on alone. It managed to survive that first rapid but not the next, where it capsized and filled with water. Normally, a canoe capsizing in fast water results from it encountering a rock. The canoe will then turn its open side towards the current, thereby filling the canoe with water which anchors it solidly in place.

June 7. I decided that I would attempt to rescue the canoe.

With my come-along, 60 metres (200 feet) of sturdy rope, and a life-jacket, I walked down to the river at the rapids where the canoe was stuck. This particular rapid is full of rocks. If one wants to fish it, one has to hopscotch from one rock to another until one is out at the edge of the main stream. This hopscotching is tricky at the best of times. Laden with my backpack and tools, I found it all the more treacherous. However, in due course I arrived at the edge of the fast water, with the canoe on its rock some 4.5 metres (fifteen feet) farther out. Having anchored the rope to a large and unmovable rock and using the rope as my lifeline, I tried to wade out into the fast water, my plan being to secure the rope to the canoe and then return to where I had left the come-along, and then crank the canoe out of the main stream. I would be quite safe on the return, because my rope, running from the canoe to terra firma, would serve as a secure lifeline. But while I was going out to the canoe, the rope was only anchored at one end and I knew that if I lost my footing and my hold on the rope, I would be swept downstream for some considerable distance, crashing against submerged rocks along the way. Such was not the end to my venture that I wished for. When someone is alone, there is no one to witness the noble attempt or to go for help if the attempt fails. And so I abandoned my mission, repacked my gear, and headed back to the cabin.

As I write this, I am not sure whether or not I told Jeanne the story at the time. It is one thing to know that one is a fool, quite another to admit it to someone else. Of course, that is foolishness in itself, because one's wife invariably knows more about one's character than one does oneself.

I needed an afternoon snooze to recover from my morning's exertions. Then a swim in the river. The water wasn't yet quite warm enough for Jeanne to indulge in more than a quick and courageous immersion.

June 8. Roch and Paul went on their own "rescue the canoe" excursion. They were successful—but Roch did get taken down the river, just as I had feared I would be. He was a little sore in places.

Why all the effort for this canoe, one might ask? Well, it resides on a ramp at the foot of the second portage downstream from the Clubhouse. More canoes are staged at the bottom of the subsequent major portages, thus allowing members to descend the river without having to carry canoes. This particular canoe, the victim of the overturn, is a sixteen-foot, solidly built, fiber-glass model, virtually indestructible, nearly flat-bottomed affair. Immensely heavy, it was designed as a moose-retrieval canoe. Its virtue for the Club members is that a family of five, maybe six (depending upon the size of the children), can be transported in it without fear of capsizing, so long as one has the skill to dock it at the head of the downstream rapid.

June 9, 10, 11. A trip to Montreal, me for the dentist, Jeanne for her hairdresser, and for bulk supplies.

We returned to our parking area at 18:00 on the 11th, only to be greeted by clouds of ravenous mosquitoes. Jeanne fled to the cabin. I did three trips with my packframe. Scooter was pleased to see us. No sign of stress. She spends a good part of any day and

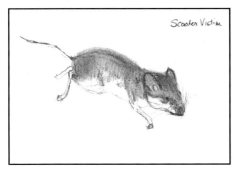

Scooter Victim

the whole of her night outside. With all the predatory wildlife around at night, we are astonished that she survives. She is, however, a very careful animal, and we think she spends most of the night sitting on her platform at the head of her outside ladder, from where she surveys her world. However, we often awake to find her offerings to us—partially eaten animals, at the foot of our bed.

June 12. Our 49th wedding anniversary.

We went into La Tuque for supplies and had lunch at Le Boké, a new bistro-style restaurant which rivals anything Montreal and Quebec City have to offer. It became our lunch stop on all of our subsequent sorties, except on Mondays, when it is closed. A plus is that Le Boké acquired what had been until then our favourite restaurant, Le Restaurant Amalthée, where Giselle and Véronique produced (and now continue to produce at Le Boké) superb modern-style, locally sourced, healthy food. Le Boké has, as a result, two menus to choose from: the more robust and very popular offerings of Le Boké, and the lighter and exquisitely tasteful offerings of Amalthée. La Tuque is a town with a number of good restaurants serving everyone's taste, from the hot dog emporium at the entrance to the central part of the town, to delicatessens, pizza places, Italian-style restaurants, and, of course, purveyors of the classic hamburger/cheeseburger/poutine fare.

June 13. Very wet. In fact, it has been raining steadily for three days. A moose yearling walked right by the cabin this morning.

June 14. Still raining.

Jeanne planted the vegetable gardens. I built log surrounds for a cucumber bed and tacked wire mesh between two trees for the vines to grow on. We walked the river round, which we generally take on rainy days as most of it is in the woods. Of culinary note, supper was of one of Jeanne's gourmet dinners: curried scallops with lime and coconut accents.

June 15. Barometer rising.

We continued planting: cucumber, basil, chives, tomatoes, pole beans, carrots, onions, spinach, lettuce, beets, Swiss chard, parsley, peas, garlic, Brussels sprouts, sunflower, nasturtiums, marigolds, blueberries, dill, rosemary, tarragon, mint, and rhubarb. Not all of these plantings succeeded. The reason for the failures was, we think, a lack of sufficient protection from the wind and, in the case of the rhubarb, soil which was too acidic. Trilliums fading, bunch berries carpeting the woods, lady slippers peeking through.

Above, left: Red Trillium.

Right: Lady Slippers.

Bottom left: A sketch of White Trillium.

Food provisioning in the Laurentian Shield is a far cry from the same activity in the southerly parts of Quebec, particularly La Montérégie and the Eastern Townships, which are regions that produce, distribute, and market locally the freshest food in North America, much of it organic. The organization Solidarité (Les Amis de la Terre), with outlets in Sutton, Cowansville, Bromont, and Waterloo, to mention only those in close proximity to Brome, is a finely tuned, user-friendly vendor of the freshest of foods, weekly, year-round. One orders off the Solidarité website which, in turn, hosts the websites of the contributing farms and market gardens of the immediate region. If one is ordering weekly, as we do when living in Brome, one selects from the producers' websites no later than Monday for pickup at the Solidarité outlet on the Thursday afternoon of the same week. One's custom-filled orders will have been picked and assembled by the producers on the Wednesday and delivered to the outlet on the Thursday morning. Talk about freshness. Talk about convenience. Talk about the essential gifts of life. Talk about buying locally and thereby preserving a local agricultural community.

In the woods, we are not so fortunate but we make do. In the land of the Laurentian Shield, with a thin layer of topsoil, if it can be called that, above the underlying shelf of solid rock, and a growing season of only four months (and even that might be optimistic), there is little encouragement to garden, but this means that those who do are dedicated to the task. These precious few do find pockets of arable land in the valley of the St. Maurice River, and the quality of what they produce is outstanding. We found Monica, who grows organic vegetables and raises organically fed chickens and, thus, organic eggs. On the meat side of things, the lamb and pork products are of the highest quality and can be obtained from the excellent butcher at the Restaurant Boké. Lamb from the Migneault farm is as good as any we have ever tasted.

The market garden in the Village of Lac-Édouard started to sell fresh vegetables in 2014, and once a week it delivers pre-ordered paniers to La Tuque from the back of a truck. Also, from June through September, Marc and his daughter, Alexandra, operate a farmers' market in La Tuque. In the very early morning, Marc drives to Yamachiche, near Trois-Rivières, a distance of some 150 kilometres (93 miles), to pick up the produce and then return. They are ready to serve at 10:00 a.m. The most recent development, much to Jeanne's delight, is the opening this year of a bulk health food and natural products store.

7

Summer 2014

June 16. Bear.

On our usual walk down to and along the river and back, a black streak flashed across the path in front of us, with a series of grunts coming simultaneously from the edge of the woods. The streak was a bear cub. We moved cautiously forward and saw the mother bear. We stopped in our tracks and remained still. I will not say that we were not nervous. We were, of course, but we knew that as a first reaction to encountering a bear one should make no sudden or violent movements. What one does if the bear approaches or attacks is another matter—which, fortunately, we did not need to figure out because mummy and baby bear disappeared into the woods. With hearts pounding, we decided not to continue with our customary round that day and instead we returned to the cabin.

Scat.

"What about bears?" was probably the most frequent question we received, but in all my perambulations in the woods, whether in Quebec, the Rockies, or elsewhere, while I have seen many bears, I've successfully relied on the basic common sense approach: "Do not move." This is backstopped by the knowledge, which one hopes is true, that the bear is more frightened of you than you are of it. Hence, the best course of action is to show no aggression or fear. Of course, there is the oft-repeated maxim: "Never get yourself between a mother bear and her cub," which I consider to be rather ex post facto advice. We often see bear scat on "our" road and we are particularly conscious of the need to make noise. I tend to sing, Jeanne wears bells on her wrists, and we both carry whistles.

June 17. Walked up our road to Clubhouse Road. Bear tracks, moose tracks, fox tracks, wolf tracks, and the scat of all.

What an exciting and invigorating time of year! The wild raspberry bushes are in full bloom, promising an excellent crop.

Bear track.

June 18. Walked to Cedar Landing, which is at the foot of the "long portage," to harvest cedar needles for Jeanne to make cedar jelly.

June 19. A cool and windy day. We kept both fires going all day, something we have not done for a while.

June 20. The usual sortie to La Tuque with the promise of a "Boké" lunch.

We had a good discussion with Gaston at the Tremblay building-supply store as to the best method of insulating the underside of the floor of the cabin. I returned with the trailer loaded with mineral wool and Tentest. That trailer has done us noble service, particularly given the beating it takes on the 411 and on "our" road.

June 21. Spent the day under the cabin on the insulation project. Mosquitoes and deerflies reign, but fortunately not under the cabin.

(For the next sixty days of the diary notations, readers may assume that I spent part of each and every day under the cabin.)

June 23. The male loon is calling consistently, signalling the attack of a predator, normally a bald eagle. The loon is aided by our resident herring gull, which makes direct attacks on the eagle. The gull wins the fights but the eagle will be back to try again.

June 24. The eagle is back. Same routine of loon calling and gull attacking eagle, this time dive-bombing it.

I went up to the Echo Rapids to fish. No luck. Chub (*gougeon*) only. Once the chub are hitting on everything one casts, one knows that the trout fishing will not be productive on the river. This is not necessarily so on Lac de la Grande Baie or Lac-Édouard in deeper water. Jean-Pierre Fournier landed a three-kilogram (6.5-pound) speckled last week, a rare catch, but one which clearly shows that the big ones are still there. The big ones are the prime regenerators, which is why the Club members release them. A speckled trout is at its best when eaten within twelve hours of being taken. Any later, and the taste diminishes. Freezing them only leads to disappointment at a later time.

June 30. Following Eugenie Bouchard's and Milos Raonic's progress at Wimbledon. They are both in the quarterfinals.

"Following" means checking the live scores on the "net," given that we do not have a television.

July 8. Ordered hemp, to be picked up near Drummondville, to be used to supplement the insulating material under the floor.

Hemp is much cleaner to handle than mineral wool and more rigid, so it can be inserted between the floor joists without it falling out before the Tentest is installed as the subflooring to hold the material in place. Had I been able to find a sufficient quantity of hemp, I would not have used mineral wool at all.

July 11. The official "Year" being over, Jeanne now permits herself to leave the sanctuary of the cabin to make sorties back to the big wide world.

We needed our snowshoes to be restrung with gut. We prefer the traditional type to the more modern metal-and-canvas models. The only people who still do this work, we found out (thanks to a reference from L. L. Bean), live south of Barre, Vermont. We used this as an excuse to take a trip.

It is a pity that in Quebec (not that this is a uniquely Quebec phenomenon), one can no longer find the artisans who used to do such things as restringing snowshoes. Try and find someone to repair a wood-and-canvas canoe. Good luck! Fortunately for the Club members, Roch and Paul still do this particular work. If it were not for them, I do not know what we would do. Canoes over the past few decades have been made in a procession of metal, fiberglass, and synthetic materials, this largely to meet the demand for sport canoes, but none of them is as comfortable to paddle as the traditional wood-and-canvas models. For us, it may be just a question of aesthetics and an attempt to keep things as natural as possible. Occasionally, however, someone will say to me: "That's a Chestnut canoe, isn't it? I used to have one but could not find anyone to repair it."

Years ago, on a cross-Canada trip on the now-nonexistent Canadian Pacific Railroad (CPR) passenger line, we spent a few days in Thunder Bay, where the Hudson's Bay store was stocked with locally made artisanal products. I vividly remember the pair of sealskin boots that Jeanne bought there and wore for years. They finally wore out but we could not find a replacement. We still have our handcrafted moccasins and use them on our snowshoes, but we will not be able to replace them when, eventually, they wear out.

July 14. A day of recovery from our trip to Vermont. The loons are with chicks on river. No sign of the eagle.

July 18. Dan Newton, with his dog Friday, dropped by on his way into his cabin on Lac Castor. He suggested a down-the-river trip for the next day.

July 19. The downriver trip is always a logistical puzzle but worth every minute of the planning and the effort.

Jeanne and I drove the truck with the canoe on the rack to Le Relais, which is on the river. We left the canoe there. This would

David and Jeanne on a Jeannotte River excursion. Photo Dan Newton.

cut about an hour and a half off the trip, most of which would have been portaging. We then drove to Lac Castor, picked up Dan, his canoe, and Friday, and drove back to Le Relais, where we launched the two canoes into the fast-flowing water, paddling for twenty minutes or so until we came to the site of the Club's cabin called "Lafleur." This cabin is the third to occupy the site. The original Lafleur cabin was a log structure built by the Lafleur family of Montreal in the early 1900s. Eventually, due to lack of use and care, it rotted and fell to the ground. Lafleur 2 was a simple and unappealing plywood structure built by the Club in the 1970s. It went the way of Lafleur 1. Lafleur 3, built by Roch and Paul, is of sturdy frame construction, well insulated and equipped with a small propane stove for cooking, a woodstove for heat, a basic kitchen with utensils, a solar-powered pump which brings up water from the river, a woodshed, and, of course, the mandatory outhouse. It is ideal as an overnight location for the fall fishing further downstream and is a convenient luncheon stop for down-the-river excursions.

Approximately 3.5 hours later, depending on wind direction, one arrives at beautiful Lac Castor. Along the way, there are two rapids to shoot (or to portage around) and countless birds to be seen on the river or in the marshes: mergansers with chicks, herons, great horned owls, cedar waxwings, and gray jays, often called Canada jays or whisky jacks. (The whisky jack will come to anyone proffering a sip of the liquor.) One also sometimes sees moose. One thing that one rarely sees is anybody else. After a fine outdoor camp-cooked meal chez Dan, Jeanne and I paddled to the landing, with Dan following. Dan then drove us, our canoe on the roof, back up to Le Relais, where we had left our truck. Dan came back with us to our camp, spent the night, and left the next day after having helped me put up our new tent, selected and sent to us by Patrick and Stephanie.

The next day Marc Fecteau, our neighbour on Lac Elie (the man previously mentioned as the firewood saviour), dropped by with his wife, Chantal, son Samuel, and daughter Noraine to pay us a visit and to send an e-mail to his brother, André, who was coming up the next day. We see Marc, André, and their families

Lakeside guest bedroom.

each summer. We also see them with their father when they come up in September to prepare for the moose-hunting season in October.

> **July 21.** Roch, David (his 2-metre [6'4"] grandson), and Paul arrived to commence the redo of the roof so as to increase the insulation and arrest the condensation forming on the underside of the ceiling in the winter.

> **July 22.** Roof work continues until noon. Temperature of 33°C [91°F] makes it impossible to work on the metal roof.

> **July 23.** Roch, David, and Paul arrived at 06:30 to take advantage of the cool of early morning. Good progress is made. Visit from André Fecteau with his wife Chantal (yes, the brothers both have wives named Chantal) and daughters Amélie and Catherine, and Samuel. It is a much cooler day, with a high of 22°C [72°F]. There are very few bugs. Jeanne and I walked up our road and I had a huge feed on raspberries.

July 24. Roch, David, and Paul arrived at 06:30. We think they will finish the roof tomorrow. Another raspberry feed.

July 25. No, they did not quite finish the roof today. That will happen tomorrow, and then we will start the cleanup.

July 26. Cleanup. Jeanne tackled the inside, I the outside. By mid-afternoon we had completed the task. We are confident the roof will be just fine.

To celebrate, we took two bottles of Mike's Seyval-Chardonnay up to the Fecteaus and had a delightful afternoon with them, sipping wine on their floating dock. Amélie and Catherine were making dolls with strips of variously coloured wool.

July 27. Sylvie and Yvon's wedding.

I met Sylvie and Yvon as a result of my having become a member of the choir. I couldn't contemplate returning from the weekly and other practices at night, especially in the winter, so Karine, the choir director, canvassed the choir for suggestions as to where Monsieur David might stay on choir practice nights, preferably for free. Sylvie Dagenais, a contralto, offered a room in their establishment, "La Résidence," a Youth Hostel.

Yvon Crevier and Sylvie Dagenais' wedding.

My first contact with Yvon was when we were returning from a visit to Brome on January 11, 2014. The drive had been difficult due to very icy roads. When we turned off the paved road onto the 411, which immediately slopes downhill, the truck simply slid all the way to the bottom of the hill. Continuing on was out of the question. Turning around and getting back up the ice slide was another thing entirely, but we made it by locking in the four-wheel drive and proceeding as slowly as possible. I had the telephone number of La Résidence with me. I phoned and a male voice answered. I asked if Sylvie was there. The answer was negative, but the man answering, no doubt detecting my accent, asked if I was the choir member who was going to come and stay with them. I answered in the affirmative and he said that we could come immediately and stay until the road was sanded. We went over to La Résidence, where I met Yvon. Jeanne had met Sylvie previously at the choir concert, and this second meeting was the beginning of a close friendship, many meals together, Jeanne and Sylvie collaborating in their artistic pursuits, Sylvie assisting Jeanne at the annual La Tuque art symposium, me find-

ing out that Yvon is a Crévier born in Senneville, where we used to live (small world). All of that developed over time but led to their enormous generosity of our being invited to their wedding, an event punctuated by the fact that by then they had been living as a couple for twenty-three years.

Weddings in our Anglo tradition can be rather staid affairs. Not so in the French-Canadian tradition, which reflects their unabashed enthusiasm for life. We knew no one apart from Sylvie and Yvon, their daughters Rose and Mathilde,

Sylvie Dagenais, painting workshop at the cabin.

and two choir members—Anthony, a tenor, and Virginie, his wife, a soprano.

We looked around for a table to sit at and were invited to join cousins of Sylvie: Oliver Loebel, his wife Lyne (Sylvie's cousin), and their children, Saskia and Yannick. They live in Brussels. I had a lively conversation with Oliver, which improved when Lyne asked why we were speaking to each other in French when we were both more fluent in English. And speaking of conversation, I had thought that Saskia and Yannick were very quiet. It was only when they went up to the front to play a musical tribute to Yvon and Sylvie that I realized that they had been preoccupied until they had delivered their delightful performance. Oliver and I have kept up an occasional correspondence ever since, this as a result of his acknowledging every one of the *Tempo* articles which I sent out electronically to those who would not receive the print version.

Many of the guests had prepared presentations, musical and otherwise. All were excellent. It was a joyous and memorable occasion. We stayed overnight in La Tuque and returned to the cabin the following morning.

July 29. Joined Michael and Soline at the Clubhouse.

Dan Newton came up for supper and joined in an interminable game of Risk in which I finally surrendered my rapidly depleted armies and then went to bed. We had three days of big breakfasts, lots of games, many excursions, and fine suppers. Mike had to leave for a day (he left at the crack of dawn but was back for supper, having resolved the problem: a fungus outbreak at the vineyard). It was a long day for him, with eight hours of driving.

August 1 and 2. Jeanne and I stayed on at the Clubhouse to greet Sylvain Gingras and his wife, Christiane, he being the very well-known chronicler of the history of the fishing clubs of Quebec, she being the photographer and proofreader of his books.

Sylvain Gingras and his wife, Christiane.

Sylvain is a fund of historical knowledge on the subject but had never before visited our club. He had contacted the secretary of the Club, Richard Riendeau, and Richard suggested that I was the person to contact. I had read his book *Un siècle d'histoire: Chasse et pêche au Québec* (*A Storied Century: Hunting and Fishing in Quebec*) which was published in 1959. He was now on a mission, some forty-plus years later, to bring everything up to date. They spent two days with us at the Clubhouse. They were delightful and fascinating guests. At sunrise on the second and last day of their stay, Sylvain and I, at the break of dawn, paddled, and portaged on an excursion downriver as the mist lifted off the water. We returned in time for breakfast, after which they departed to go to La Seigneurie du Triton, mentioned earlier in this book.

August 5. Intense concentration on the insulation project beneath the cabin.

I commenced the installation of the four-by-eight-foot sheets of Tentest so as to close and seal the inserted rows of hemp and mineral wool. It was quite a trick to install panels of that size while lying on one's back. How I learned to do it was to lie on my back and pull a sheet of the Tentest up and over my body as if I were pulling up a sheet in bed. Then I would position it, as accurately as I was able, directly under the floor joists where it was to be installed, grasp blindly for my electric screwdriver, insert a screw onto one corner of the panel and screw it part way into a joist. Once that manoeuver was accomplished, I adjusted the position of the panel with my legs, arms, and feet until it was, as far as I could judge, directly under and in line with where I intended it to go. I screwed a second screw into the opposite joist and then squirmed my way feet first under the rest of the panel until I was in place to install screws in the other two corners. I now had a panel, no longer being supported by my body, hanging loosely from where I intended it to go. I then started back at the first corner, tightened the screw, did the same to its opposite screw, and went along installing further screws, moving from one side of the panel to the other, until I reached the two screws I had installed at the other end of the panel, adjusting them so that the panel would be tight and flat against the joists over its entire length. I repeated this process over the next few weeks until all the boxes were completely sealed by the Tentest, eighteen panels in all. Then I covered them with wire mesh where they abutted each other, so as to be sure that mice and squirrels would not make their winter homes in the construction.

Enough of this subject. I eventually completed it on October 4, the day after my seventy-fourth birthday. Having written all this, I now realize why I hate written directions: I can never follow them and I wonder if you have been able to follow this one.

During the course of the day, Jean-François Bilodeau, his wife, Brigitte, and their delightfully active four-year-old son, Simon, dropped by for a visit. They were staying at the Club.

At the end of the afternoon of August 5 we decided not to go into La Tuque, as we had previously planned, to take in the summer Thursday street concert, this week featuring Robert Charlebois. We just did not feel like making the effort. In hindsight, I regretted our decision. However, cocktails on the porch, while watching the setting sun after a very physical day, seemed at the time to be an irresistible alternative. We phoned Le Boké to cancel our dinner reservation. I learned later that our cancellation allowed another couple to enjoy its fare and that Le Boké served a record 140 people that evening. The "entire" town comes out for these summer "*jeudi*" (Thursday) concerts, and Le Boké's terrace is right on the main street where the performances occur.

August 10. Roch and Paul completed the remaining details of the new roof. The cabin is now truly a four-season dwelling.

The balance of August blessed us with consistently beautiful summer weather, which we enjoyed as summer vacationers at our wilderness abode. We were satisfied that we could now face the winter with confidence in our heating stoves, the beneath-the-floor insulation, and the insulation of the new roof. We swam daily, canoed to Jake's for the annual blueberry pick, picked and ate raspberries on our walks, and paddled and portaged up to the Clubhouse to enjoy cocktails with Dick and Amie Riendeau, Jacques and Chantal Laurin.

Labour Day weekend arrived and was consumed by continuous heavy rain. The Pagé family from the environs of Trois-Rivières came up, as usual, to camp and fish on this holiday weekend. Discouraged by the weather, they did not last past Sunday.

September 2. Mike arrived having delivered 68 cases of Les Pervenches wine to the restaurants of Quebec City. We had a far-ranging conversation on life, goals, options, and aspirations. Each year he becomes more confident in the vineyard as he and Véronique annually sell out their entire stock.

September 3. A large bull moose, with full rack, swam slowly across the river in the direction of Lac de la Grande Baie, stopping to eat the water plants when he reached the shallow water near the shore, eventually moving off into the woods. A magnificent sight.

After this treat, Mike and I set off on our annual late-summer fishing exploration of the river. We never expect to catch much at this time of year. It is simply the pleasure of once again being together, reliving memories, and making new ones. Jeanne followed us down the river, stopping at favourite spots to read. Jeanne and I went back to the cabin in mid-afternoon. Mike continued with his explorations. As we returned to the cabin, a ferocious tornado swept down the river towards the cabin, snapping off the tops of medium-size balsams. As luck would have it, nothing hit the cabin but there was a tangled mess left to clear. We were worried for Mike being on the river but he arrived back oblivious to what had happened.

September 7. Late afternoon I went to try my luck in the river, it being the last day of the fishing season.

I stayed off the river until I knew that all the Club members had finished their fishing weekend. After all, I can go fishing anytime I like during the season. (Not so the Club members who come up only for a weekend here and there.) I got lucky.

Devastation.

8

Autumn 2014

September 10. First choir practice of the new season, the majority returning from last year and a number of new people.

September 11. Supper conversation turned to how much longer we would stay at the cabin.

The plan had been to spend one year in the woods. We were now at fifteen months. Should we sell our house in Brome and live here for as long as we are physically capable? No conclusion reached.

September 12. Geese flying south. Covered the tomatoes to protect them from the possibility of an overnight frost.

September 13. High of 7°C [63°F]. More geese. The hummingbirds left a few day ago.

I used to tell Steph and Mike, and then told Daphne, Soline, and Cedric, that these tiny birds could not possibly migrate all the way to southern Mexico and Central America all by themselves.

That is why they disappear when the geese start going south: they hitch a ride on the backs of the obliging geese. I will have to find new victims for my tall tale.

September 14. Sortie.

Our adventure in the woods was never intended to be an abandonment of everyone we knew and loved, but it certainly was a separation, distant and dramatic in concept. However, having closeted herself for "The Year," Jeanne was eager to re-engage herself with family and friends, and to test whether or not she wanted to return to our home in Brome. Therefore, we planned the following excursion:

(1) Visit with our tenants Luc and Sylvie Robert.

(2) Lunch with our neighbours, Jean-François Doré and Nicole Bélanger.

(3) Move in the direction of Toronto, ultimate destination the Stratford Festival, where we will be joined by Steph, Daphne, and Cedric.

(4) Go to Oakville to spend a night with brother Jonathan and his wife Marnie.

(5) Continue on to Stratford.

(6) Visit with Colin McAlpine, Jeanne's brother, and his wife Sandy in Orangeville, Ontario.

(7) Go to Perth, Ontario, to stay with Bob and Barb Mingie, high school friends of Jeanne whom we try to visit very year.

(8) Stay with Monique Yates in Knowlton.

(9) Schedule dentist appointments in Granby.

(10) Stay at Hovey Manor in North Hatley, where Jeanne waitressed during summer vacations and where, in 1965, we held our wedding reception after the service in St. Mark's Chapel at Bishop's University, where we met and fell in love some fifty-four years ago.

(11) Attend our class reunions at Bishop's—mine, class of '62; Jeanne's, class of '65.

(12) Meet with clients and friends in North Hatley.

(13) Stock up with supplies in Sherbrooke, and

(14) Return to the cabin.

During our absence, Nathalie Bergeron and Richard Delisle kindly dropped by the cabin to visit and feed Scooter. In addition, Roch and Paul were there for three days doing this and that.

Sept. 28. Upon our return to the cabin we discovered a pile of kindling cut by Richard. Roch and Paul had completed most of our list: caulking the perimeter of the floor to prevent the ingress of cold, and felling a dead tree which might, at some point, have fallen upon the cabin. We sat on the porch of the cabin and luxuriated in being "home" after a marvelous twelve-day sortie.

The Year Became Two and Then Became Three

When we met with Luc and Sylvie Robert in Brome at the beginning of the trip, we mentioned that we might put the house up for sale. Luc kindly said he would not object to having a real estate agent and prospective buyers visit the house. His lease would end in April 2015. Upon our return from our trip, he phoned—knowing, we think, that we were not certain of our future living plans—and said, "Instead of selling your house, why not think of renting it to me for another year, until April 2016?" Jeanne had no immediate answer for Luc. However, after revisiting the subject of what we were going to do upon our exit from the woods, we decided to postpone the entire discussion. Jeanne phoned Luc and extended the lease to April 2016. Thus, the "Year" in the woods would become "Three." With a great sigh of relief from both of us, the dilemma was resolved, at least for the next year or so.

September 29. The weather has collapsed to rain, rain, and rain. Jeanne spent the day settling back into the cabin and giving much attention to Scooter.

September 30. Jeanne is canning tomatoes and beets, and making applesauce. Canning, I discovered, takes lots of water, hence many trips with buckets to and from the river.

October 1. 6°C [43°F] outside and 16°C [61°F] inside at 07:00, this without the fires being lit before we went to bed. That means to me that all of the summer and fall work on insulation is having its effect.

October 2. A memorable fall day. Mist rising off river in the morning and then full sun. Outside temperature reached a high of 20°C [68°F].

In the afternoon, we walked up our road and saw three partridge within a space of 100 metres (about 110 yards). One was sunning itself on a south-facing bank. It was not six metres (twenty feet) from us but did not move and showed no sign of fear at our presence. Another took flight with the usual *brrrrr*. The third wandered up the track in front of us, pecking at this and that. It eventually walked into the woods and disappeared from view. Upon returning to the cabin we observed the two baby loons, now not so small, on the river, and also mergansers. A hawk alighted on the ground in front of the cabin, and a robin, a rare sight, was perched in a tree.

October 3. Birthday (David) greetings received from the family. Errands in La Tuque. Lunch at Boké. People delighted that we are staying until April 2016. Upon return to cabin, took down and stowed tent. High of 18°C [64°F].

October 4. Up early, as usual. Emptied the ash trays of the stoves, laid and lit the fires, waited until they were both going well (a matter of some twenty minutes), brewed a pot of coffee, adjusted the flues on the fires, put the two-gallon pot on the cookstove to heat water for dishwashing. Then outside to the woodshed to replenish the inside supply of wood, swept up the ashes and pieces of wood resulting from my fire laying and wood fetching, carried water from the river, pausing as always to survey the scene, cleaned up any dishes left over from last night's supper, had a cup of coffee, laid the breakfast table. Now it is 05:45 and light outside. Stacked the last of the outside piles of split logs into the woodshed and chopped kindling. Somewhere around 06:45, went back inside to check on the fires and to see whether there was any sign of a stir from the bed and, if so, deliver a cup of coffee to the occupant, which is a sure way of anticipating breakfast within the next hour or so. Wrote up my diary. I love this daily routine. The break of dawn is such an exciting and invigorating time of day.

There is an adult loon on the lake with two chicks, but these are not our annual summer residents. This we could tell from the very small size of one of the two chicks. We surmised that this was the family of the loons we had observed on Lac de la Grande Baie in the summer. We do not see how the smaller of the two chicks would be ready to fly south by the end of November / early December. The mother is still feeding it.

During the course of our sojourn in the north woods we received many questions concerning loons. Apart from answering them as best we could, we referred the questioners to Joan Dunning's book, *The Loon: Voice of the Wilderness*. It is sensitively written and beautifully illustrated.

A heron alighted in the trees above our dock and stayed for a while before moving on to its nesting site. There was significant action on the spawning beds. Overnight temperatures are now flirting with zero degrees.

October 7. Walked our usual round down to the river, down the portage, back up to the parking lot, and back to the cabin. At the river, we observed the frenetic activity of the mating season. Huge trout were lunging, surfacing, and cruising the pool as if involved in a major military exercise. At 18:00, heard wolves howling from the rise of land to the north side of the river, to be answered from the other side. This went on for about thirty minutes and then silence. Moon almost full.

October 10. Hunting season is open. The occasional rifle shot heard. Geese constantly overhead. Barred owls calling. Wolves howling again. Full moon.

October 11. Mounted wall bracket above propane tank. I needed it to assist me in hoisting propane tanks up and onto the platform, where they are connected to the regulators.

David with his new come-a-long.

This was quite the exercise. The bracket was made for me by Denys Duchesne at Pro-Mec Élite in La Tuque. I found it too heavy to lift and hold in place in order to bolt it to the wall of the cabin. Perched on a ladder, I was not feeling secure in what I was doing. Jeanne was watching the exercise with her usual trepidation. She resolved the problem by pointing out that the swivel arm, the heaviest part, from which the come-along would be hung, could be detached from the body of the bracket. I detached it accordingly and was able to complete the job.

Having bolted the bracket to the wall with six-inch bolts, using my new Makita cordless power hammer drill, I reinstalled the swivel arm and hung the come-along on it, but then found that the chain was not long enough to reach the propane tanks lying at the foot of the slope. So I attached a rope to the chain and tied the rope to a tank. Now I was in business. It took me a few tries to perfect the technique, but the objective had now been achieved and has worked ever since.

October 12. Checked secureness of the wooden ladder on the roof, which allows me to climb up and clean off the solar panels in the winter. Attached security rope. Last winter I regularly shoveled the snow from the roof, but was often dealing with ice. With the new insulated roof, I was hoping that the task would be easier. No gunshots today. Walked up our road wearing our fluorescent caps and vests. No sign of Mr. Faucher, who has a blind on our road adjacent to the path to Moose Swamp. Perhaps he was successful and went home.

October 13. Left camp at 08:45 for La Tuque to fetch Laura Hernandez, who has come up from Knowlton to visit.

Laura Hernandez, doing her morning yoga on the tent platform.

Laura is an expert in homeopathic cures (she's a disciple of Mikaël Zayat, the guru of essential oils), an artist, a dancer, and a yoga teacher. She emigrated from Mexico City with her Canadian husband to Canada to help his family, which had opened a now very successful fasting clinic in Knowlton. Laura is no longer involved with the clinic, having decided to open a yoga studio. Because of Jeanne, I have been privileged to meet the fascinating people who inhabit the sensitive world of the spiritual and artistic communities.

October 14. Paddled and portaged to Lac de la Grande Baie, Laura taking pictures. A high of 16°C [61°F]. Cocktails on porch.

October 15. Laura is leaving today. We drove her back to her car in La Tuque. Laura was a very special guest. We hope she finds time to visit again.

October 16–18. Continuous rain and warm temperatures until the evening of the 18th, when it stopped raining and began to blow, with the temperature dropping rapidly. We could smell winter. Scooter sensed the change and has gone into hibernation. She has begun the big sleep of her long winter. The change of the seasons at this latitude, at least in respect to temperature, does not conform to the recognized official dates of the change of the seasons. What feels like winter here comes well before December 22 and lasts well past March 22, the official first day of spring.

October 19. Geese overhead. Snowing.

We have no intention of manicuring the forest around us. However, inevitably with the strong, sometimes fierce and occasionally tornado-force winds, stuff does come down, particularly the tops of balsams. The paths need to be kept clear. Thus, I am constantly picking up branches and cutting up larger falls. I keep anything of size to split into kindling and toss the rest on one of my three brush piles. The safest time to burn is when everything is covered in snow.

October 22. Choir practice. Had supper with Yvon and Sylvie, who instructed me on my plant-watering duties at their home, which I will perform during the winter on choir practice days. Yvon and Sylvie will be in Thailand for the winter. I will stay overnight at their home on choir practice nights.

October 23. To Montreal on business.

What a shock to find oneself on access roads jammed with creeping vehicles, thirty or more kilometres (twenty or more miles) from entering the downtown area. Then, in the city, finding not a single road which is not cluttered with construction pylons and detour signs leading often, or so it seems, to nowhere one wants to go. Quite a shock to go where millions attempt to live together—as opposed to La Tuque, where I have never encountered a traffic jam. Jeanne came along to attend to business, banking, etc. Business accomplished, we were happy to be going back to our life in the woods. On the drive back, we tried to guess what the inside temperature of the cabin would be. We guessed 9°C (49°F). Both nights had lows below zero and highs of only 12°C (54°F). In fact, at 18:30 the inside thermometer showed 14°C (57°F). The summer's insulation projects work.

October 25. Paddled to the Echo Rapids and walked up the trail to winterize the canoe we leave at the head of the portage so that, in the non-winter seasons, we do not need to carry it up and down the portage.

Winterizing a canoe in the forest, as I learned from Roch, means standing it on end and securing it to the trunk of a medium-size balsam, the branches of the tree serving to protect the canoe from the snow. This is the method that Roch used for all

How to store a canoe in the woods in the winter.

of the Club members' canoes—that is, before the Club invested in the construction of a canoe shed. On the way back, we slowly paddled around the bays and then over the spawning beds where the mergansers were diving, all under a warm fall sun. In the early evening, we sat on the porch and discussed the magic of living here amongst the trees and the energy they extend to us.

October 30. No more geese? No sign of the loons. Mergansers on lake around the spawning beds. Maybe the loons are up on Lac de la Grande Baie making group travel plans with the rest of the gang. Installed tarpaulin on west side of woodshed to stop snow from entering.

October 31. Did not reload furnace fire before going to bed but shut it right down. In the morning, nine hours later, I did not need a match to restart it.

November 1. Geese and more geese. Mergansers.

In the afternoon, went to visit Jacques Giroux, exiting the 411 at km post 18. Jacques has been a constant fund of knowledge on how to live comfortably in the woods. He has been particularly helpful on the subject of the solar system.

November 3. Planned an ambitious walk. Up our road to the trail leading into Moose Swamp, then following the trail to and past Moose Lake and up onto Road B, as it is called. (Road B runs parallel to the road which I call "our road.") Then turning right and coming to the washed-out area where the beavers have built a metropolis of dams, ditches, banks, and slides. We call this domain "Beaver City". The beavers, with their

Beaver lodge.

Beaver dam activity creating a pond behind the dam.

ingenuity and determination, put us humans to shame. When we decided to live in the woods for a year, it was our hope that we would really explore the forest. However, it took us until now, our second November, to have the time to indulge that wish. Now that we feel the cabin is secure from all points of view, we are looking forward to exploring the inner sanctums of the woods.

November 4. Counted 30+ male hooded mergansers on the river.

November 6. Into La Tuque to have winter tires installed. We have been concerned that we have not seen the loons for a while. Today we heard one single, solitary cry. Was it a "goodbye"?

Oil painting, *Echo Point Cabin*, by Jeanne Marler.

November 7. With Jeanne's help installed the winter tarpaulin around the perimeter of the crawl space beneath the cabin.

November 9. Walked with Jeanne back up to Road B but this time turned left, in the direction of the river.

Our plan was to see if it would lead us to Jacques Fournier's moose-hunting swamp area above Echo Point Cabin. If it did, we would have a way to reach the Clubhouse on snowshoes, thus avoiding Clubhouse Road, which, in the winter, is a dangerous snowmobile highway. However, the trail petered out. I still think there must be a way, but since then we have not been back to try again.

After the walk, I took my big chainsaw up to the Chaloupe Bay track and felled four medium-size *merisiers*, blocked them into eighteen-inch (big stove) lengths, and stacked them preparatory to fetching them once there is enough snow to operate the snowmobile. I was determined that we would not, once again, run out of firewood, and further determined that if I was going to live in the woods, I should be able to look after myself. And so commenced a winter adventure of getting the snowmobile stuck and spending the rest of the day freeing it. The ratio of stuck time to productive wood time was probably 70:30.

November 15. Today's walk was a favourite but with a new dimension.

We took the trail that leads to the river, and then, having passed the old hunting camp, we turned away from the river and ascended a wide gully. The gully itself is very open and studded with enormous *merisiers*. It had not been touched since the days of the forestry cut in the area, which occurred some twenty-plus years ago and which had taken only softwood. I determined that this would be the place which would supply our firewood for the winter of 2015–2016. I would, in the interim, widen the trail to it so that I could access it and bring the firewood back, using my snowmobile.

The river was substantially frozen over. Two hooded mergansers were in the open river channel. Otherwise, it was a quiet scene devoid of other birds, although I am still not sure whether the baby loons have departed.

November 16. −6°C [43°F] 07:00. Snowed all day, melting on the ground.

November 18. To Granby for a dentist appointment.

Quebec now decrees that one must have installed one's snow tires by December 15. Why so late, I do not understand. Invariably, the first dump of snow occurs in November. It usually melts away over the following two or three days but it nearly always causes havoc. Today was such a day. The ditches were strewn with cars, some abandoned, some with their occupants in them, waiting for a tow truck. The waits must have been long. I navigated cautiously, but the all-wheel drive made me feel relatively secure in my truck. I arrived very late at Mike and Véro's for supper.

November 20. Return to La Tuque and cabin.

The 411 had twenty-plus centimetres (eight inches) of unplowed snow on it. Once back at the cabin, I decided it was time to move the truck to its winter parking place at Le Relais. We did not want to risk not being able to get it there. First we went to La Tuque, then returned with the snowmobile, which had been in La Tuque for a pre-winter checkup. Cautiously, we returned to the cabin on the snowmobile. I say "cautiously" because there was not enough snow to be sure that the machine would clear all the rocks along the way. There certainly was not enough snow to take the machine all the way to the cabin. We left it at the traditional parking spot, 350 metres (382 yards) from the cabin. For the time being, we could move our provisions on a hand-pulled sleigh. Once the fires were lit we felt snug and secure and ready for the joy of real winter.

> **November** 21. 11°C [52°F] at 05:30. Three trips on the snowmobile to Le Relais to retrieve from the truck the balance of yesterday's provisioning, including a full propane tank. After lunch we took our usual daily walk. It was not easy. Not enough for snowshoes. Very mushy and slippery in our boots.

Here is the text of a piece I wrote for *Tempo* entitled "The Woods, Health, and Time":

I have remarked in previous articles on my joy in being so fit and healthy, and Rob Paterson, the webmaster of the *Tempo* online site, has asked me to write upon the topic. It has taken me some time to figure out how to approach the subject, because I would like it to have relevance to my readership. Not everyone wants to or is able to live in a wilderness situation. What I decided was to simply write what works for me and to let you decide what may be of relevance to you.

It occurs to me that the key ingredient to a healthy life is having time. The absence of time causes stress and stress is debilitating.

As a youngster at school and then at university, I was very physically active. At school, outdoor activity and sports were a part of the daily curriculum. At college, they were part of our social life. I then arrived at law school and subsequently into the practice, as it is called, of law—and I ran out of "time." Physical activity was not part of the curriculum. Of course, I could have elected to play sports and remain physically active, except that the pressure of study and then of work was the priority. This was not because I chose it to be so but because of the way it was determined to be by the college courses and then the employing law firm.

At the beginning of any day I had to get to work, whether by bus or by car, and at the end of the day I was exhausted by the unremitting desk job and had neither the energy nor the inclination to go to a gym or engage in physical activity. On entering law school I weighed, at 1.8 metres (six feet) tall, 66 kilos (145 pounds). On exiting law school and having successfully completed the law society entrance exams, I weighed some 81.6 kilos (180 pounds). Over the years, the weight increased to some 98 kilos (220 pounds) and I gained a pot belly which my granddaughter, Soline, thought indicated that I would soon be producing a playmate for her to enjoy.

Throughout the period of some forty-five years of weight increase, I continually told myself that I must join a gym and eventually I did. I paid my year's subscription and rented an executive-style locker which I stocked with everything necessary for the training and post-activity showering. I invested a chunk of money into my health and conditioning program before I had even put on my pair of the latest (and socially mandatory) training shoes. I might have started at the gym the following day, except that I had a breakfast business meeting or a partnership meeting or brief I had to get out. I did not have time to go to the gym that day. I would go tomorrow, which became tomorrow and then tomorrow and then. . . .

When I eventually went back to the gym, my key would not open my locker and I was told that the lockers get cleaned out if membership is not renewed annually. Annually! That meant that I had done no organized, regular exercise for over a year. And so I decided to walk to work and walk to the court and walk to meetings outside of the office. But then, one morning I had an early breakfast meeting, and at lunch time it was raining or snowing or too slippery, and at seven o'clock in the evening, when I could have gone to the gym, I remembered that we had a cocktail party to go to, and then, after that, we went out to a restaurant with friends. In the morning, I was too tired to walk to work. I just did not have time to exercise.

This problem—not to mention the fact that the baby never came though the "pregnancy" increased—was that I started to feel increased levels of stress when I became fifty-something years of age. I told myself firmly that if I did not do something about this right away, I would die an early and uncomfortable death. And I reinforced that stressful notion when I arrived at sixty years of age. But meanwhile, I still did not have time.

David, preparing to carry a battery to the cabin.

Fortunately, there was Jeanne. She had given up on the exercise thing for me but not on her longstanding plan that we would live in the woods before it was too late. Jeanne is a patient person— but don't push it. In due course, she wins. And so off we went to the woods.

This environment dictates, if one is to survive, that substantial parts of every day involve physical activity. Yesterday, just as an example, I made four trips on foot in 20 centimetres (eight inches) of fresh snow to retrieve things from the truck. So that was 8 × 350 metres = 2,800 metres (1¾ miles). The trips included a "100-pound" propane tank which actually, when full, weighs eighty-four kilograms (185 pounds). I loaded it onto a sled. (There was not enough snow to use the snowmobile.) Pulling the sled and tank uphill was a pull-pull-and-pull exercise. Going downhill, the trick was to get out of the way of the descending torpedo. Then I had to install the tank. Once that was accomplished, I went back up to the truck to retrieve various items which I brought back on my packframe.

A packframe is a structure made of vertical and horizontal steel tubes which hangs on one's back, as does a packsack. At the bottom of the structure there is a platform made of the same tubes. One starts by setting the unloaded frame on something which is at the same approximate level as one's waist. I use the tailgate of my truck. One then stacks boxes or bags or whatever one has to carry upon the platform, one item on top of the other, strapping the load to the upright part of the structure with bungee cords. One then slips one's arms through the carrying straps, tightening them just as one would a packsack. Then one just walks to wherever one wants to go. One never has to lift anything from a non-horizontal position, thus there is no strain on one's back. When one gets to where one wants to go, one needs a convenient balcony or stool on which to sit before one extracts one's arms from the carrying straps so that, again, one never has to bend over—because if one did, the weight of the load would probably make one fall flat on one's face.

Then I attend to wood management, bringing in wood for the cookstove and for the heating stove. Following which I fetch water from the lake. In the winter, this activity requires chopping the ice to re-open the hole. Also in the winter, I may need to climb up onto the roof to clear the snow from the solar panels. (Don't worry. There is a ladder secured to the roof and a rope with handholds attached to it. But yes, one has to be very careful.)

These tasks, all pleasurable, some challenging, sometimes amusing, take about four hours. At about 15:00, according to our daily routine, Jeanne and I go for a fifty-minute walk through the woods and along the river. Thus in one day (and most days are the same), I am engaged in approximately five hours of physical activity.

Jeanne has always has been very fit as a result of her days as a competitive swimmer and gymnast, and her career as a dance teacher. Such a life required that she have an advanced knowledge of the human anatomy as it relates to physical fitness. She pointed out to me that exercise classes at a gym are designed to work every muscle and limb of the body, and that I, in my daily routine in the woods, am unconsciously giving myself, in an atmosphere of enjoyment and challenge, intellectual as well as physical, at least as good a workout as I ever would have had at the gym—and, what's more, this comes at no cost.

I have wondered what it is about the woods that makes me feel so healthy. A friend of ours, a guru in all things natural, wrote to Jeanne and said: "When I saw David recently he looked well" (a polite way of saying, "He's lost weight").

November 23. Warming trend continues. −2°C [28°F] at 06:00.

I carried the chainsaws and the related equipment to the gully. It was a treat to work in this location. Firstly, it is a five-minute walk from the cabin and would, once there was sufficient snow base, be less than that by snowmobile. Secondly, because of the maturity of the *merisiers*, there is very little growth beneath their canopies, which meant a relatively limited clearing operation around the base of any tree to be felled. The trees I selected were of medium size. I did not want to bring down the big ones because they are the seed distributers for the future growth. Also, I did not have nor want a chainsaw big enough to cut trees of very large circumference, because the more powerful the saw, the heavier—therefore more tiring, therefore more dangerous. I have a medium-large Jonsered for the medium-large work, and a Husqvarna 440 for branches and smaller work. I wear professional logger's chaps, steel-toed professional logger's boots, goggles, earmuffs, and a helmet. I am very aware of the dangers, particularly when cutting alone. Roch and Paul do the big stuff. My cutting is supplemental.

I split the logs by hand. I use a splitting maul and sledge-hammer to make the initial split, and the maul alone on most of the subsequent splits. Sometimes the maul will not penetrate the wood. It simply bounces back. In such cases, I start with an axe. Once I have driven it in an inch or two (2.5–5 centimetres) with the sledgehammer, I withdraw it and substitute the maul. If one drives an axe in too far, it becomes very difficult to extract. One often reads of the use of metal wedges. The problem with them is that they are the devil to get out of the log if one does not succeed in splitting it. The splitting maul, on the other hand, is a wedge on the end of a handle. The handle allows one to work the head of the maul free of the log.

Splitting an annual supply of twenty-plus cords by hand is a monumental task. So why not use a gasoline-driven splitter? This gets me back to time considerations. If one is a professional firewood provider, one uses the machine because time is money. Equivalently, if one does not have time because of the pressures of life, splitting any considerable quantity of wood by hand is not feasible. However, if one does have the time, as I do, there is nothing more satisfying and healthy than splitting by hand. There is the satisfaction when the log eventually splits open. There is the fact that one does not need gasoline. Using a power-driven splitter always carries the risk, as one loads a log, that one's fingers will not be extracted in time from the approach of the splitting blade. But above all, at least for me, splitting wood is a physically rewarding exercise. It is in the great outdoors. Nature surrounds one. That is what we came here for.

November 28. Opening the hole in ice for the retrieval of water.

This is a tricky exercise at this time of year. One needs the water—but is the ice thick enough to hold one's weight? Not the end of the world if it is not, because at the beginning of the freeze-up, I cut the hole near to shore.

November 29. Walked up the road. Tracks of moose, deer, fox, hare, and (perhaps) a wolverine.

It is generally true that moose and deer do not make good neigh-bours. The primary reason may be the ticks that deer carry, which are detrimental to the health of the moose. I am no expert on the subject, and, as with everything about our decision to live for a period in the woods, it is all on a continuous learning curve. However, from the point of view of our own observations, there is no doubt that the deer population is increasing. Seeing a deer in this territory used to be rare. But during the past ten years or so we have become used to seeing deer once we are close to La Tuque. We have also seen deer tracks on our walks. Every year the number of sightings increases. There is no deer hunting in this region for the moment, but the opening of a deer-hunting season is said to be imminent.

9

Winter 2014–2015

❦

December 2. The first truly cold night of this winter: −22°C [−8°F].

December 4–8. A major renovation task designed by Jeanne is to enlarge and make access easier to the mezzanine (loft). Roch, Paul, and Roch's son, Pierre, his wife, Anick, and Roch's grandson, David, were the team, with Jeanne, the designer, supervising every detail.

Roch is an experienced contractor. Paul has the eye of an artist and his working with logs produces results of great sensitivity and

Enlarging the loft.

Above: Romeo and
Juliet balcony.

Left: New stairs to
loft to replace original
ladder.

.

beauty. Pierre is a professional builder. Anick is a successful entre-
preneur in her own businesses. David is immensely strong and
logs are immensely heavy. Anick and I had the job of de-barking
the balsam trees which Paul had felled for the supports and stairs
of the project. They were a superb team and the results speak for
themselves. The concept was, firstly, to enlarge the loft in order to
provide an area for Jeanne to use as an art studio; secondly, to make
access to the loft easier by building a log staircase (access up until
then having been by a ladder) and then to turn the loft halfway
across the south wall so that we could have access to open, shut,
and clean the windows in the eaves without needing to fetch the
extension ladder, as we did before. This walkway was relatively
narrow and therefore needed a railing which, once installed with
Jeanne standing proudly behind it, evoked the image of Juliet on
her balcony.

Roch and the team stayed at the Clubhouse, commuting to us
daily by snowmobile.

It was during this project that I learned that *merisier* burns
wet. Up until then, the wood we were burning had been cut in
March. By the time the following winter arrived, the wood was
dry, having been stored in the woodshed. The trick is to get the
fire going well with dry wood. After that the fire will quickly
ignite the green wood, which will hold all night. The danger
in using wet wood, particularly softwood (from conifers such as
balsam fir), which except for kindling we were not using, is that
wet wood exudes creosote, a potential fire hazard if allowed to
build up in the chimney. Such a buildup is partially avoided by
burning with a hot fire. With our very cold winters, we are almost
always burning hot. Our subsequent annual fall chimney clean-
ings revealed virtually no creosote buildup in the chimney of the
heating stove and only a little in the chimney of the cookstove.

On the Scooter side of the news, she hates renovations or
any disturbance to her abode or way of life. She disappeared for
the duration of the project, sometimes underneath the covers of
our bed, sometimes secreted somewhere in the loft. Only Jeanne
could find her.

December 6. I am now using the snowmobile daily to fetch wood from my November cutting in the gully and then splitting and stacking it. I could still use more snow to cover all of the thin parts on the trail and on our road, but day by day the tracks are firming up.

December 7. Jeanne's birthday.

The construction team, of which I counted myself part, sang "C'est à ton tour" to Jeanne. "C'est à ton tour" is the song that French-Canadians sing to celebrate a birthday. We delayed the dinner celebration until the 9th so as to be able to enjoy ourselves in a dust-free environment. It took us two days to clean the cabin and put it back in order following the completion of the renovations. As usual, we served ourselves rack of lamb, the lamb coming from the Migneault farm in La Tuque, purchased from Le Boké. Succulent it was, as always, and enhanced by a bottle of Les Pervenches pinot noir.

December 8. Choir practice in La Tuque for the upcoming concert. Back at the cabin by 22:45. Increasing snow depth is making the snowmobile run easier.

December 11. First snowshoe sortie of the winter on three inches of freshly fallen snow. Sunset at 16:45.

December 14. Concert with Marc Hervieux.

The concert was a great success. The church was full. I felt exhilarated from the first note to the last. We were back at the cabin, no snowmobile mishaps this time, at 23:00, after a choir supper at Le Boké. While coming down our road, we had slowly followed a mature bull moose, keeping our distance. He finally turned off into the woods just before the place where we turn off onto the trail that takes us to the cabin. I was somewhat concerned that we would meet him again while we were going in, but we did not.

December 15. Followed yesterday's moose tracks on our snowshoes on the trail down to Chaloupe Bay and found his bed.

December 16–28. Both out to Montreal: legal work for me, hairdresser for Jeanne, overnight stay with Danny and Seana; to Barre, Vermont, to pick up our snowshoes; to Montreal Airport, staying overnight at the Marriott in preparation for an early-morning flight to Thunder Bay, via Toronto, for our annual Christmas visit with Stephanie and family.

During this absence, Paul stayed at our cabin to keep Scooter company (they are good friends) and to accomplish certain renovation tasks. We returned on the 28th. No more snow had fallen since we left. Paul met us at Le Relais. He then walked to the Lafleur cabin, some 500 metres (approximately a third of a mile) away, where he had left his snowmobile, and we took ours back to the cabin.

While we were away, Paul had oiled the downstairs floor, put a preservative cover on the new logs in the recent renovation, and installed new pine frames around the doors and windows. Scooter was happy and pleased to see us. I really felt that we were coming home—not just coming to our cabin.

December 29. A day of catching up outside. Replenished indoor wood supply, cleared snow and ice from solar panels and from the roof ladder, roof-raked the east-side deck roof; snowmobiled to the truck at Le Relais to retrieve what we had brought back with us, other than the perishables which we had taken in yesterday. Went back for propane cylinders which we had picked up in La Tuque. Snowshoed the river round. Fetched water from the lake.

January 1, 2015. Happy New Year.

Raking the snow off the roof.

Opened up a snowmobile trail down to the river, along the shore and then back into the woods to join up with the track which brings one to the gully where I have been cutting wood. The track will not be useable for transporting the wood until it has been well tracked, tamped down, and frozen. I will run the snowmobile over it for a number of days before testing it with a load of logs.

January 2. A morning acknowledging the e-mails commenting on my articles. It is gratifying to know that there is an engaged readership.

January 3. Further chainsaw work on intended snowmobile trail to gully.

I was able to run the snowmobile over the track down to the river and along the river but was unable to get it up the steep pitch from the river to the top of the bank which leads to the gully. So I turned it around to drive it back up the bank which I had descended to get to the lake. I didn't make it. I then spent the afternoon winching the snowmobile up the bank with my trusty come-along and rope. I resolved to do more preparatory track work on snowshoes before again trying the snowmobile.

January 6. −33°C [−27°F] at 06:00.

January 7. The usual chores which now include almost daily climbs onto the roof to clear the solar panels.

Fortunately, the climb is up the east side of the cabin. Thus, I am sheltered from the frigid west wind blowing in from across the frozen river—that is, except when I stand up to sweep the panels or scrape them (in the case of ice).

January 8. Solidly in the deep freeze at −35°C [−31°F].

January 9. Snowshoed the river round at −28°C [−18°F]. It took thirty minutes for my fingers to warm up. I looked at my intended snowmobile trail to the gully and decided to wait for more snow. Going over it daily on snowshoes is building it up and hardening it.

January 13. Snowshoed up the river to the Echo Rapids, then up the portage and back.

Going up the portage through deep, fluffy, untracked snow was hard work. On the way back, just below the rapids, there was a small hole in the ice which rarely closes, this because of a rock just below the surface of the water. Here we found the scat of an otter and the remains of its meal of fish.

January 19. Temperature at 05:30 −1°C [30.2°F] in anticipation of a forecasted dump of snow.

It came and dumped a welcome twenty centimetres (eight inches). Good for my snowmobile track to the gully project. The problem was that I had to start by going down to the river without any guarantee that I would be able to get back up.

Guy Roy came over and made it down and back up. Of course, he has a superior level of skill. I declined to try myself while he was there because, if I were to fail, I did not want to hold him up in an attempt to get me back up. He said that he would come back the next day and that we would take both his machine and mine on a trial run. Meanwhile, I have still been cutting in the gully and have at least two cords to bring back, if ever I can get to them.

January 20. Partial success.

Guy and I took our snowmobiles over to the gully. He then gave me a demonstration of operating a snowmobile in unpacked snow. He climbed part way up the gully on his machine, moving very slowly, always standing up so as to be able to move his weight, backwards and forwards and side to side as required, demonstrating that slow and easy does it.

After he left, I drove my machine back to the cabin and hitched on my sled with the plan of making a run to the gully to retrieve a load of wood. All went as planned until I tried to get back up the slope to the cabin. No such luck. I detached the sled and let it slide back down to the river. I took the snowmobile in reverse down to the river, unloaded half of the wood from the sled and then attempted to get back up the bank with the half-load. No such luck. So, I again released the sled and let it slide back down to the river. Then I again drove the snowmobile backwards down and was successful in then driving it back up—but, of course, without the sled. I resolved that I needed yet more snow on the bank. Guy had also said that I should investigate a more consistently level approach to the gully, but that was not something which I could feasibly do until the summer.

January 21–23. In Quebec City on business.

January 24. I decided to try again to bring the wood up the bank from the river. I shoveled snow onto the slope, tamped it down with my snowshoes and repeated the exercise three times. I then gently took the snowmobile down the track, turned it around and as slowly as possible drove it successfully back up. Eureka! I went back down and hitched on the sled with the half-load that I had not been successful in bringing up previously. It took some doing to free the sled from the snow and ice where it had sat for the past four days. Once that was accomplished I tried to get up the bank. This time, again, Eureka! I spent the rest of the day fetching half-loads and so gradually started to achieve my objective: becoming potentially self-sufficient from a firewood point of view. I now also had logs to split and stack.

Jeanne's Voice from the Woods

I have been lucky enough to have had some very special experiences in my life. The time spent in our log cabin in the woods is certainly one of them.

But why? Why is it so wonderful to have to go to the outhouse when it is −25°C (−13°F), to take sponge baths instead of hot showers or real baths, to have to lug a full knapsack of laundry to the laundromat fifty kilometres (thirty miles) away, and to prepare three meals a day from scratch? No pizza delivery here! We don't even have a physical address. Just GPS co-ordinates.

Wilderness has been part of our lives since our twenties. For me, every time we had to come home, I could only think of all the reasons not to leave. Now I don't have to leave—a dream has come true. I have always cherished the times in my life when I have had time to just be, time to run outside and take a picture of the loon babies or a beautiful sunset, time to sit in the warmth of the March sun on the south side of the cabin and read a book, time to keep in touch with friends, time to paint.

Okay, enough of this idealistic, Pollyanna stuff. Living here in the woods has its responsibilities. David has kept you abreast of his part. So what do I do here apart from running outside with my camera to capture David on the roof, David chopping wood, David chainsawing, etc.?

I figure that it takes me four to six hours a day to look after all the meals (I try to limit grocery shopping to once every two weeks), keep the cabin in shape, and repair anything which might be broken. (Thank you, *Martha Stewart Living* magazine, which taught me how to repair a wiggly chair.) An unexpected challenge arose when the door handle fell out of one of the outside doors on a day when it was −20°C (−4°F). I now know how door handles work.

Many people ask about our water, or should I say, the lack of running water in the cabin. It means that we have developed strategies to use as little as possible. After all, David has lugged each drop in a bucket, up from a frozen river. My game is to see how many times I can use a cup of water. For instance, I start by rinsing the broccoli sprouts which are growing in a quart jar. I use that same water to cook the carrots for supper. If there is any water left when draining the carrots, then it is used as water for porridge the next morning.

Another water question has to do with showers and baths. I am happy taking sponge baths, but have to confess to looking forward to the times when we go back home or to Montreal so that I can fill the bathtub, put in a few drops of essentials oils, and submerge myself in the steamy, aromatic water. Washing my hair in a bowl in the sink is the water challenge I find most difficult, and it uses so much water if I want to do a proper job and get all the soap out of my hair.

Cooking on the wood-burning cookstove requires getting used to, but once mastered, it's wonderful. Bring the pot of rice to a boil on the left-hand/hot side of the stove and then just move it to the right-hand/less-hot side for it to simmer quietly until cooked. With the large heated surface of the stove, I happily cook pancakes in the huge cast-iron frying pan; the same for canning in my large canning pot. I pop plates into the warming oven above the stove to heat them, and I dry herbs in there, too, at no extra effort. Oven fries are delicious cooked in the woodstove oven, crispy and full of flavour. Brome Lake duck breast, too. Now, it is difficult for me to imagine working in a kitchen without a wood-burning cookstove.

Laundry Breakthrough

For the first two years of our sojourn in the woods, doing our laundry at the laundromat in La Tuque was, shall we say, a pain. Sometimes we had to wait for a machine to be free, but, admittedly, we needed three laundry machines to deal with our every-two-week, sometimes three-week, loads. There was the question of timing, specifically getting to the laundromat early; otherwise our day in La Tuque could become very long. Then there came a point when we learned that the laundromat was going to close. What to do? We might have contemplated doing our laundry in the river, except that would have been an impossibly cold exercise in the winter, or, alternatively, would have required me to make untold numbers of bucket trips. Making those trips on Jeanne's hair-washing days was one thing, in respect of which I had no choice. For laundry water those trips would need to be substantially multiplied. And, in any event, we would not have tolerated that the river be polluted by the detergents.

And so we consulted Nathalie Bergeron, and she found us Mme Roy, who was set up at her home to do large quantities of laundry. Then it became a simple matter of dropping off a load at her home and picking it up on our next trip into La Tuque, and simultaneously leaving the next load. Mme Roy is a perfectionist. All was immaculately clean, ironed where appropriate, neatly folded, and packed into our laundry bags. What had been an exercise of at least two hours of our time became a matter of a two-minute drop-off/pickup. Thank you, Nathalie. Thank you, Mme Roy. You relieved us of a chore which had blighted the enjoyment of our excursions to La Tuque.

January 28. Activity for today: we are going to visit Guy Roy. He has some skins which we would like to see before he takes them to the wholesaler in Lac Saint-Jean.

We set out on the snowmobile after lunch, with the temperature at −19°C (−2°F), took the 411 to kilometre 24, and then followed the track leading off to the left until we found his sign and turned into his domain on Lac-Éveline. He was there. He showed us the skins of the animals he had trapped (hare, fox, marten, lynx) and explained the process. He had also completed the construction of an insulated shed in which he stored the blocks of ice he had cut from the lake, in the hope that they would stay frozen until next year's moose-hunting season. It was a fascinating afternoon and particularly so because we saw a person who had been able to construct the life he wished, living in the woods all winter long.

January 31. Snowmobiled to Le Relais for lunch.

There was quite a crowd of people there. I chatted with Clermont Ricard, a highly respected and well-known trapper and hunter, who built Le Relais and then ran it for a number of years. When I was the president of our fishing club, he approached me to buy the lease we held on the site of the Lafleur cabin. I resisted. I had wanted to see the Lafleur camp resurrected, which, as you already know, it was, and very successfully. He respected the decision and has remained a supportive friend. When we told him in the summer of 2012 that we were intending to live full-time in a cabin on the river, he, without hesitation, showed us where he hid the key for Le Relais and how to get the heat going in the stoves, just in case we should need a refuge. That is the type of person he is, not dissimilar to the generosity of everyone we meet in La Tuque and Lac-Édouard. We felt secure in our environment, even as our friends and family back home worried about our safety.

On that visit to Le Relais, we also became aware that we are not the only couple living full-time in the woods. We met André and Lucille, who live permanently in the vicinity of Lac aux

Rognons, and they told us of a doctor and his wife who live on Lac Caribou.

February 2. Full moon tonight and a cold one, going down to −33°C [−27°F]. Clermont will be trapping wolves. After tonight, if successful, he will have met his quota. He will then concentrate on the preparation of his pelts to go to the wholesaler in Lac Saint-Jean.

While I was snowshoeing up our road, a tiny shrew jumped onto my snowshoes and then ran up my leg under my overalls. I shook him out. Maybe I should have kept him and taken him back for Scooter. Either way, poor shrew.

February 4. While I was away on business, Jeanne saw two moose browsing on our road.

February 6. −34°C [−29°F] last night. We installed cold-weather screens.

These screens, if that is what they can be called, were designed and constructed by Jeanne. They consist of wooden panels covered with felt on the side facing the doors and windows. Clips on the doors and windows hold them in place. We also install them when we leave the cabin for any protracted length of time so that the contents of the cabin are out of sight and therefore, we hope, out of mind to any snooper who might happen by, however unlikely that might be. The images below are facings on the panels which cover the kitchen windows. They are the creations of Daphne and Cedric.

February 6. We have, as previously discussed, been supplementing the wood supply cut by Roch and Paul last March. I have been cutting since mid-January. We are rapidly consuming the wood cut last winter by Roch and his team. However, I now have a frozen track to the gully and

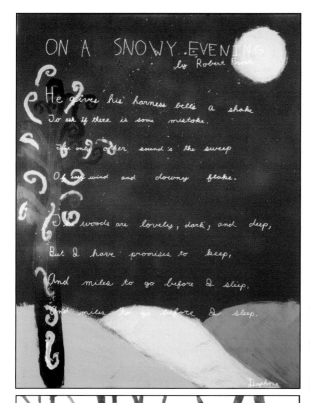

Window panel. *On a Snowy Evening*, poem by Robert Frost, created by Daphne Martel, our granddaughter.

Window panel. *Stopping by Woods*, poem by Robert Frost, created by Cedric Martel, our grandson.

am fetching a sled load or two of *merisier* per day. We will be fine until Roch and team arrive for the annual March cut.

February 8. −27°C [−17°F]. Having difficulty in getting the heat up in the cabin, no doubt as a result of this continuing frigid spell, this notwithstanding the one balmy day with a temperate high of −13°C [9°F]. We both have colds, our first since being here.

February 9. We slept in the loft last night. Refueled stove at 03:00 and again at 07:00, at which time the exterior temperature was −28°C [−19°F]. Up to −12°C [10°F] in the afternoon. No wind. Continued cutting. Three sled loads to woodshed. No snowmobile adventures.

February 10. Are we through it? −13°C [9°F] at 07:00. Up to −8°C [18°F] in the early afternoon. Snowshoed the river round. We are both feeling better. It is said that last winter was one of the coldest on record. This one is colder.

February 11. Phoned Guy Roy. I could not start the snowmobile.

David and Guy Roy, our trapper friend.

Soon after I called, Guy came over and fixed the problem: spark plugs. He is such a help and emergency backup for us. Without him being so (relatively) close, we would feel much less secure. Along with our thanks, he left with a freshly Jeanne-baked loaf of date bread. On his last visit, he left with a tin full of chocolate bark. I have no reason to feel jealous, because Jeanne always makes a double—one for me—of whatever she makes for Guy.

February 14. −32°C [−26°F]. St. Valentine's Day. Dinner: a rack of Le Boké lamb and a bottle of Mike's pinot noir. Still sleeping upstairs in loft.

February 16. Two moose on our road.

February 17. −33°C [−27°F]. Large moose tracks by rock not 100' [30 m] from cabin.

Our increasingly precarious wood situation led me to wanting to bring my chainsaws into the cabin to unfreeze them. This was not approved by Madame. So I went into La Tuque where, at Canadian Tire, I bought a propane-driven heater which I installed in the cupboard of the woodshed. That did the trick. Within half an hour or so, the saws were operational.

The nights were becoming more moderate, with temperatures in the minus teens. And, at the risk of repeating myself (although now in a positive direction), it is remarkable how the interior of the cabin eventually responds to the outside temperatures. Once again, I think we will survive. Meanwhile, I would have to keep cutting. But just a few days later and we were back into the deep freeze with temperatures at −°30C (−22°F) or lower.

March 8−16. An outing for legal work in Montreal.

During our absence, Pierre and Anick were at the cabin and looked after Scooter. They always come with three or four dogs. Scooter stays in the loft. They are accomplished wilderness people. Pierre brought in with him a gasoline-driven auger to increase the size of our water hole in the ice. It had become so frozen in that I could barely get to the bottom of it with my axe to let the water rise into the hole. We arrived back to a warm and spotless cabin.

On Anick's departure her snowmobile left the track—at a difficult spot, one which had caused me problems until I figured out exactly how to navigate it. The two of us extracted the machine, with me pulling with my machine. I have to admit to have had some satisfaction in knowing that even the pros get themselves stuck from time to time.

And then the winter trials were over. The days intermittently brought in torrents of snow but with moderate temperatures. March certainly is one of the finest months to spend in the woods: warm afternoon sun on clear days, lengthening days, rambling snowshoe adventures on a hard crust of snow, northern lights on clear nights. It is as if we were on a winter vacation.

At Home in the Woods

March 17. We are OK for wood. Roch and team will be in for the major spring firewood cut in the next few days.

April 3. Danny and Seana arrived for the weekend.

And talking of visitors during the depth of winter, we never knew when Denis and Véro might appear for a visit from Lac-Édouard by snowmobile. When they came it was always with an edible gift, whether a cut from a moose shot in the hunting season, or a partridge or hare shot on their way to us, or one of Véro's other culinary treats. Each time they also told us how to prepare and cook their offerings. (See the "Recipes" section following the Postscript.)

April and the first half of May are, perhaps, the most difficult months to spend in the woods. The snowmobile track progressively rots away, and the road would be ruined if we drove the truck to get in and out. Further, as recounted in the spring of 2014, the 411 becomes exceedingly treacherous and unpredictable. We abandoned snowshoeing on April 12 when the night snow crust ceased to form.

On the same day, the roof released its snow load in one spectacular avalanche. We had been anticipating the event and were very cautious and careful when going into or out of the cabin. I spent the afternoon, with Jeanne's help, putting back the ladder on the roof. It had come down, unscathed, in the avalanche. Not so the aluminum ladder which I use to get onto the roof. Its base being frozen in a solid block of ice, it snapped at the fourth rung from the ground, leaving that part firmly stuck in its snow anchor for a few more weeks. However, the balance of the ladder was still long enough to serve the purpose of getting me onto the roof to clear the solar panels.

Notwithstanding the road conditions, I felt that I must get myself to the last choir practice before the spring concert. I had been going in as regularly as possible during the winter, staying at Sylvie and Yvon's, with the duty of watering their plants while they were away in Thailand. Going to that choir practice meant walking out and back from Le Relais, five kilometres (three miles) in each direction. Nevertheless, I was as fit as I could possibly be after a winter of opening the ice hole for the water in the lake, carrying up the buckets, splitting firewood, carrying firewood, and climbing up to and down from the roof to clear the solar panels of ice and snow, as well as my extracting-the-snowmobile adventures—though, I am happy to say, these gradually became the exception rather than the rule.

And so we returned to the cycle of life of living in the woods for another year: the excitement of spring with all that it brings, including the birds, the fishing, the paddling, and, eventually, the swimming, the return of the Club members, the enjoyment of seeing them and listening to them recounting their escapades.

The loons returning on April 28, the same date as in 2014.

That the cabin has no civic address caused us a number of interesting problems. It is not on a municipally recognized road; indeed, it is on no road at all and, therefore, has no street number by which it can be identified. We were blithely ignorant of the complications that this phenomenon would cause. In this digital age, one is frequently called upon to provide, along with such other information as is requested, one's address. Not having one often means that one can have difficulty in accomplishing one's online objectives. Bureaucracy cannot cope when an item required by a list cannot be provided. We could insert our GPS coordinates, I suppose, but that would not be accepted as a "valid response."

Our first encounter with this phenomenon was in receiving parcels sent to us by courier. For our address we gave the address of the La Tuque Post Office, where we had a mail box. However, when a courier attempted to deliver to the Post Office, it refused to accept the parcel. Solution: our always-ready-to-help Nathalie Bergeron. She kindly agreed that we could give her address to the company from which we might be ordering. This, of course, was to the mutual advantage of both Jeanne and Nathalie, as it meant more visits and more chats *chez* Nathalie, by reason of our having to pick up our parcels at Nathalie's house.

The second encounter concerned the renewal of my permit to practice law. From time to time the Quebec Bar Association (Q.B.A.) sends an inspector to the office of the lawyer so that it can be sure, from a face-to-face meeting with the lawyer, that all regulations concerning the lawyer's practice are being observed. In 2014, I received an e-mail from the Q.B.A. informing me that an inspector, name and coordinates provided, would conduct just such an investigation, and inviting me to arrange with the inspector a convenient day and time for him to visit me at my office. I e-mailed the named inspector, stating that my office was temporarily situated in a remote location northeast of La Tuque. I gave him directions from La Tuque to Le Relais but with two caveats. Caveat No. 1 was that he have a four-wheel-drive vehicle with high clearance. Caveat No. 2 was that he should dress as if he were going on a trek in the woods, which he would be, and that, if in the period of late May–end of July, he should equip himself with bug repellant. I never heard from him again. My license was, nonetheless, renewed.

The third encounter was in respect to voting in the 2015 Federal Election. Jeanne and I went to the polling office in La Tuque, well before voting day, to ask whether we could vote in La Tuque. We were in the process of giving our names when the person to whom we were speaking, recognizing our accents, called for the English-speaking person required at every polling station. She came up to the counter and introduced herself as Mrs. Bachelder. This was one of the very few times during our three-year sojourn that we were spoken to in English. I was about to tell Mrs. Bachelder that we preferred to speak in French but then realized that she was just doing her job, and I thought it would be rude not to speak to her in English because we were, perhaps, her only chance to do her job.

She asked us for the address of our current residence. Our inability to provide same, not having one, was, understandably, beyond the experience of the local polling station. We gave our e-mail address and telephone number and were told that we would be contacted by the "head office," which in due course we were. The man calling said: "But one must have a civic address in the electoral district in which one wishes to vote." I replied that we were not prepared to go and buy or rent a dwelling for just one day in order for it to masquerade as something which it would not be, to wit, our residence. "And anyway," I said, "if we were on vacation in some foreign part we would be allowed to vote 'remotely'—and yet here we are in La Tuque, which is still in Canada, being denied the most fundamental of our democratic privileges." The gentleman to whom I was speaking was sympathetic and said that he would see what might be done.

Some few weeks later, on one of our La Tuque days, we dropped by the polling station to see if it had received any clarification of our status. Mrs. Bachelder was delighted, I would say even excited, to inform us that we were on the voting list and that the advance poll was open.

We voted.

❦

Summer 2015

This year, the visit of Michael and Soline coincided with that of Stephanie, Daphne, and Cedric. No Patrick this year. Someone has to work! The highlight was our river trip down to the Lafleur cabin. Mike and the children went in one large and indestructible canoe called the *Yellow Submarine.*

"Down the River" trip. Daphne, Soline and Michael.

Jeanne, Steph, and I took the portages using the staged canoes. We met up at the bridge above Le Relais from where Steph, Mike, and the children swam, propelled by the current, down to the Lafleur cabin. Jeanne and I paddled, serving as lifeguards— quite unnecessarily, as we expected would be the case.

The difference between this spring, summer, and fall from the two preceding is that I had no major project that required my attention. Insulation of floor: done. New roof: done. Root cellar: project abandoned. In all other respects, the daily routine

Grandchildren, jumping off the Clubhouse wharf.

remained the same. It was a memorable three seasons—exactly the type that, when one is city-bound by one's job, one dreams of as a paradise. And it was.

The one major addition to our experience was Jeanne's taking part in the 2015 annual La Tuque art symposium. By participating in it, she became a participant in La Tuque, and more and more we became part of the town. But this only added angst to our discussions of what we would do in and after April 2016, when the lease on our home in Brome would expire. This question became a constantly recurring subject of discussion.

I am looking at my diary page for May 7, 2015. It has a heading "Advantages/Disadvantages: Cabin/Brome." But the list tells one nothing, for each place is special and to select one means the sadness of abandoning the other.

However, we had another winter yet to come, that of 2015–16. The two previous winters were a matter of the survival of two people who, by and large, had to learn on the job. Somehow we did, and not the least of that was because of the support and advice we received from so many. Those two winters rank amongst the coldest on record for La Tuque and Lac-Édouard. If we had been forewarned, I like to think that we would, nonetheless, have proceeded with our plan. Had we been forewarned of the winter to come, that of 2015–16, I am not sure we would have renewed the lease of our house for that final year.

Fall 2015

An addition we made for our final winter was a workshop, designed by Jeanne, attached to the back of the woodshed by Roch, Paul, and Jean-Pierre Fournier. My primary objective was to have a place to properly organize and keep my tools, with a stove—our original too-small model, which would allow me to thaw out my chainsaws and be warm while I sharpened them. Roch and Paul also installed a composting toilet in the new workshop.

Roch Lepage, Jean-Pierre Fournier and Paul Bérubé, in front of the new workshop.

But, as before, my primary concern was wood for the cook-stove and, more importantly, for the winter heating stove. In this respect, I was greatly and enjoyably aided by Jacques Émond, one of my choir buddies, who volunteered to come in and help me fell and block trees (*merisiers*). In preparation, I cut the track that Guy Roy had suggested; it would lead from the cabin to the gully, overland, maintaining the same approximate elevation. Of course, there were ups and downs to deal with, but no dramatic slopes. The cutting and removal of the trees to make a wide-enough track, and filling in holes, took the better part of two weeks of intermittent work.

> **November** 23. Jacques arrived at 07:30 and we were under way by 08:00, each tackling a different tree. We went at it until 12:00, returned for lunch, courtesy of Jeanne, and then went back to cut from 13:00–15:00.

We will go at it again next week and, if we get as far as we did today, my concerns of running out, before Roch and Paul come in for the annual March cut, will have been dispelled.

In the meantime, I went back to the gully every day, continuing to cut. On Jacques's return the following week, we felled three more trees, and with that I considered we had reached our desired amount. From then on, I gathered the logs and stacked them into four piles. When the snow began to fall, I marked the four locations with ribbons tied to trees so that I could find the piles in the snow. By late December, all was covered in snow.

Winter 2015–16

It was proving to be a much warmer winter than the preceding two. An early winter sample shows an average difference of some five to ten degrees. This persisted throughout the winter. How pleasant, we thought. The snow came down in abundance. What is a real winter without immense quantities of the white stuff? That, at least, is what we thought at the time.

December 30. I had taken our snowmobile to Denis at Nautico for a checkup. The report came back: "kaput". I had been anticipating this.

I had a number of concerns about the machine during the previous two winters, to the point that I was not as confident in it as I would have liked to have been. Not being confident in one's snowmobile is not very comforting when one lives some fifty kilometres (thirty-one miles) from civilization. I went to consult with Denis and, some considerable amount poorer, became the owner of a 2010 Bombardier Expedition, the model he had recommended when we first met in 2013. The big differences were that it has a four-stroke engine, as opposed to a two-stroke; it starts with a key, as opposed to with a pull cord; it is more comfortable, especially on the pillion seat; and it is easier to steer. The Expedition also navigates the unpacked snow better than the Skandic, but that may have something to do with my improved technique.

Thus, I was now fully equipped for a winter of logging in the gully. I would be on a well-prepared, level trail, on a very reliable machine, and with not nearly so far to go. Further, there would be substantially more fetching than cutting, given the work that Jacques and I had started and which I had continued, and there was plenty of snow on the ground, even as early as late December, to enable me to build a solid track.

My January and February diary entries, except for intervals when I was in Montreal or Quebec City on business, and a one-week trip when we went to Mexico to see Mike, Véro, and Soline, record the collecting of the logs from the cutting sites in the gully. I was as happy as I could imagine spending my days in the woods engaged in this essential and healthy activity. I felt so much more comfortable because I knew what I was doing and knew, too, that we would not run out of wood. By early March I had moved to the woodshed all of the logs that I could dig out of the snow.

Then I started to split. *Merisier* is not the easiest wood to split by hand. However, when it is frozen it is easier than when it is not, and it splits with a satisfying suddenness.

The winter changed for us on February 12, the day when Jeanne's brother Colin died. His death was not a surprise. He had been diagnosed with cancer of the brain six years previously. It was just, as is all of life, a question of time. Thus, we needed to make plans to go to Orangeville to help comfort and assist his widow, Sandy, and attend the funeral. From our end, we needed to see if Paul was available to come and look after Scooter while we were away. That was not a problem. The problem, and a persisting one, as I am about to recount, was the ice storms, the first of which occurred on the day prior to the morning of our intended departure.

> **February** 16. Temperature rose during the day to −1°C [30°F]. Heavy snow in the morning and afternoon, turning to rain, creating a sodden mess.

> **February** 17. I awoke to survey a scene of disaster around the cabin: the tops of fir trees snapped off, the white birches cleaned of their dead branches, which littered the ground. Paul was to be at the cabin at 08:00. Today we had planned to go as far as Kingston, Ontario, which would have taken about ten hours if all had gone well. It didn't.

When Paul did not arrive by 08:30, I thought that I had better go out to Le Relais to see what was what; but I was still hoping that I would meet him coming in. When I reached our road, I saw a scene of devastation. The road was completely blocked in places by branches which had collapsed under the weight of the wet snow. I went back to the cabin to fetch my lighter chainsaw and a pruning saw and then went back up to the road to cut a way out. By about 11:00, I had cleared a tunnel through the

Ice storm. Our road, February, 2016.

mess up to Clubhouse Road, which was not as closed in as our road but was far from being clear. I cleared my way through and arrived at Le Relais at about 11:30. No sign of Paul or of anyone else. I took the truck for 200 metres (about 200 yards) or so onto the 411. It seemed doubtful to me that the road would be passable. I returned to the cabin and phoned Paul's home in La Tuque. Joanne, his wife, told me he had been delayed by trees fallen completely across the 411 and had returned home to enlist the help of his uncle, and that the two of them were in the process of cutting their way in. Armed with that information and given the long drive we had ahead of us, I decided that we should pack up and go to Le Relais and wait for Paul there. As it happened, he and his uncle arrived just as we did. He proceeded on to the cabin, I having warned him of the partially cleared state of the road.

We were on our way. It was now 13:00. I became stuck in a snowdrift about two kilometres (a mile and a quarter) out from Le Relais: the truck had ridden up on the snow as I was attempting to go around a fallen tree. I would have to excavate the entire underside of the truck, which I proceeded to attempt to do. Fortunately, Paul's uncle was not many minutes behind us on his return to La Tuque. He was driving a full-size truck equipped with all the gear, and after he had pulled our truck back onto the road he kindly agreed to follow us out. Proceeding in company in such conditions is, of course, recommended but not always possible. It was slow going but we finally reached La Tuque at 15:00, Trois-Rivières at 17:00, north of Montreal at 19:00, off the Island of Montreal and onto the 401 at 20:00. We did not get to Kingston until well after midnight because of freezing rain conditions on the 401. (Interesting how nasty roads—I am referring to the 411 and the 401—have very similar numbers.) Exhausted but relieved, we fell into bed at the first hotel we could find.

The next morning we picked up Stephanie at the airport in Toronto, she having flown in from Thunder Bay. We arrived in Orangeville that afternoon and stayed at Colin and Sandy's home, and the next day we went to the funeral and reception, which Sandy had conceived with much sensitivity. She had arranged for certain of Colin's closest friends to say a few words. My contribution was the following:

I knew Colin from my earliest days of dating his sister Jeanne, which was fifty-four years ago. He was in grade 10 at Beaconsfield High School in Beaconsfield, Quebec. I was at law school, McGill, and living in residence, as my parents were still living in the U.K. In due course, during my pursuit of Jeanne, I was invited to stay for a visit at the McAlpine home, and this became as frequent an occasion as I could wangle, for Mrs. McAlpine was a superb cook, only one of the advantages of my having found Jeanne. This was before the days when parents blithely allowed the visiting boyfriend to bunk with the object of his desires and so I slept in the spare bed in Colin's room. Colin and I quickly struck up an easy relationship. He was unassuming and always studiously involved in one activity or another, such as taking apart the McAlpine toaster to see how it worked, although not figuring out how to put it back together. But my real getting to know Colin was when Mr. and Mrs. McAlpine asked me if I would come and stay at their home and keep Colin company while they were away at a business convention of Mr. McAlpine's employer, the Sun Life Assurance Company of Canada, incidentally Sandy's employer during her business career—small world. At the time, Jeanne was attending Laval University in Quebec City. So the question was: what to do to keep Colin company on the weekend. Colin had acquired from his cousin, Fred Dodge, a Sunfish sailboat (the precursor of the Laser), and I had been a mad-keen sailor since my boyhood. So I suggested to Colin that we should take his boat out on the Lake of Two Mountains. It was in April. The ice was just off the lake. It was pouring rain and blowing hard. Waves in that shallow body of water were standing straight up, two feet high. We launched and were away close-hauled, sailing blind as the rain teemed into our faces and the water washed over the boat. What concerned me was that at some point we would have to come about to get back, and I foresaw that as a moment of terror to be encountered. Colin, at this point in his sailing career, was simply hanging on for dear life but seemed not in the least concerned. Ignorance is bliss. I had visions of drowning my (perhaps) future brother-in-law. But about we came, let out the sail, and surfed back towards the beach—when out of the murk came a magnified voice. I briefly thought that the Almighty was about to intervene, for better or for worse—but no, it was the megaphoned voice of an officer of a Canadian Coast Guard cutter telling us to return to shore immediately, which, of course, is precisely what I was attempting to do. We landed, soaked and shivering, but ecstatic from our adventure. Years later, as you know, sailing became Colin's passion, and we would join him for his Georgian Bay cruises on his yacht Dream Catcher. *The high moment of Colin's life was his meeting and falling in love with and marrying Sandy, who became his constant companion on their trips to exotic places, their annual sailing cruises, and the last six, progressively more difficult years of Colin's life. The two of them endured the experience with fortitude and always with their sense of humour intact. Colin was a wonderful person. Sandy fulfilled his life and he hers.*

Following the reception and after an hour or two back at Sandy's, I drove Stephanie back to my brother Jonathan's home in Oakville. He would drive her to the airport later that evening for her return flight to Thunder Bay. I spent the night at Jonathan's and left early the next morning to pick up Jeanne at Sandy's. We then drove to La Tuque, arriving at 22:00, and spent the night there.

The next morning, we headed back onto the 411. It was in an even worse condition than the day we had left. The snow was deep and the passageway between the fallen trees was only just enough to get through. But we made it. Paul was at Le Relais to meet us. He told us that while we were away there had been

Driving on Route 411.

another ice-/snowstorm, and that our road was at least as bad as it had been on the day of our departure. He said that he had cleared a path through the mess sufficient to allow him to get out.

When we reached our road, I could not imagine how Paul had managed to get out. In places he must have simply put his head down behind the windshield of the snowmobile and forced it through the tangles. Paul had warned us to be very careful and to stick religiously to the tracked part of the trail. I was not successful. Not far down the trail the snowmobile slid off the track and I could not drive it back on. I unhooked the sled, which was fully loaded, and used it as a sled on the downhills, dragging it, with Jeanne's assistance, on the uphill portions. It was strenuous work, but we finally made it. Scooter was happy to see us. The cabin was warm from the fire which Paul had started before he left to meet us.

February 21. The usual extract-the-snowmobile routine. Loaded my gear. Walked back up the road. Attached the gear to the machine and the end of the rope to a tree and began to winch.

Extracting the snowmobile from deep snow is a slow business at the best of times and was very slow this time. The farther the machine is from the required tree, the longer the rope, and the longer the rope, the more slack to be taken up, and once the rope is more or less tight it will start to stretch as one winches. It seems forever before the machine moves. In due course and with Jeanne having come up to bring lunch and to help, we finally had the machine on the track and headed for home. There were times in these exercises when I almost despaired of success. However, with a deep breath and a short rest I carried on.

The next few days brought no relief. The temperature remained around zero. Every morning for the next ten days, my entire time, except for the routine morning chores, was taken up with clearing and re-clearing our road up to Clubhouse Road. Not a day went by without more snow and rain falling, the rain turning to ice as soon as it hit the branches of the trees. In the afternoons, Jeanne would join me and toss the branches I'd cut free into the forest. I initially thought that I would do this all with the chainsaw. The problem was that I needed one hand to pull the branches down to where I could cut them and the other hand to pick up the chainsaw. Often the chainsaw was beyond my reach and, in any event, using a chainsaw with only one hand on it is about as dangerous a thing as one might imagine. Thus, fairly quickly I abandoned the chainsaw and used only the pruning saw. It was quick and easy on any branch of eight centimetres (three inches) in diameter or less. If I had a larger branch to cut, I would struggle through the deep snow and cut the tree at its base with the chainsaw.

This was my every day activity until March 1.

March 1. Time to re-provision.

We took the snowmobile to Le Relais. The Clubhouse Road had been cleared by some sort of machine that just plowed its way into the forest, forcing back and breaking the branches as it went. It was not a pretty sight, but the road was clear. We arrived at Le Relais, switched to the truck, and headed out on the 411. After a few hundred metres (several hundred yards), we decided that it would be very foolish to continue. Trees were down, partially closing the road. The snow was deep, wet, and heavy. We returned the truck to Le Relais and ourselves, on the snowmobile, to the cabin. It then began to snow again, requiring me to again open our road. In addition to working on the road and attending to my daily chores, I spent my time shoveling the roof and clearing the solar panels. Meanwhile we were rationing our food. When would this weather stop and when would the 411 be plowed?

March 4. We decided to try again to get to La Tuque.

One of the owners was at Le Relais. He also was contemplating trying to get out. We both decided that, having company, we would proceed, whereas otherwise we would not have. We slipped, slid, and slalomed, took hair-raising runs at the uphills and crept with extreme caution on the downs. We made it and had a conversation of mutual relief and congratulation at the La Tuque end of the 411. We agreed to meet for the return trip, and we were back at the cabin at 18:00.

That evening we had another one of our "where are we going to live" conversations. By this time, it was clear that we did not wish to risk a repeat of what we had just experienced, not so much because of what it was but because of what, in terms of result, it might have been. When one is young, one thinks of people in their seventies as being old and less physically capable. Neither of us felt that applied to us . . . but we knew that one day it would.

To add to the decision-making process was the fact that no forestry operations were contemplated for the winter of 2016–17 in the area serviced by the 411. It seemed probable that the road would be maintained by contributions from the chalet owners and the ZEC but only as far as kilometre 21, thus leaving us with nine kilometres (five-plus miles) of unplowed road to Le Relais. Also, it did not seem certain that Le Relais would open for the winter season. We did not wish to think in terms of access to La Tuque being by snowmobile on the seventy-four-kilometre (forty-six-mile) snowmobile track. The 411 was an essential, albeit unpredictable, element in our ability to live at our cabin. Not knowing for certain that we could rely on it decided the question, irrespective of all of the other considerations.

We had accomplished more than we had set out to do—spend an entire year in the woods—and I have explained how—happily for us—that one year became three. Jeanne wrote the following letter to one of her friends, Susan Archibald, who, with her husband Lew, live in a remote area of British Columbia.

Dear Susan,

I haven't been ignoring your wonderful, descriptive e-mails. I have been waiting for the inspiration to write back in the same vein. And we have been preoccupied with the question as to whether we stay here, in the woods, permanently or return to Brome. First of all, I have to say you are very insightful regarding our thoughts of wishing to stay here and the fact that I feel so creative here. Yet, our property and home in Brome is the most beautiful home/property we have owned. We renovated the house from top to bottom. It suits our needs wonderfully. The view is spectacular and the relative remoteness remarkable.

Fall colours in Brome.

We heat by wood, have a screened-in porch with a Murphy bed so we can sleep there most nights in the summer. We excavated a large pond so we can swim and it seasonally hosts migrating ducks and turtles. Frogs regale us with their musical and non-musical croaks at night. The coyotes wail. Deer and wild turkey are abundant. We have a pristine stream at the bottom of our property, berries grow in abundance. The feng shui is excellent. The list goes on. We have kept the landscaping simple so that if we want to be creative there is lots of scope for vegetable and herb gardens, fruit trees, etc. The property needs constant attention and that is something which David adores doing. There is no doubt that we will miss our life in the woods and the friends we have made. But we will keep the cabin and use it for vacations. And above all, we want to be nearer to our children and grandchildren. David has always wanted to spend time at Michael and Véronique's vineyard. And all our books and family photograph albums are in Brome. Our lease to the couple who has been renting Brome ends in April. We have decided to go home. It has not been an easy decision. Thank you for the inspiration you have given to us by corresponding from your own piece of remote paradise.

Fondly,
Jeanne

In early March I started making runs, four in all, to take our "stuff" back to Brome. Scooter knew that something was up. She hates seeing boxes and bags being packed. The snow conditions were now deteriorating rapidly and we had to get out before the 411 became impassable. Departure day was set for April 9, the day following our tenants' departure from our home in Brome. We hoped that would be feasible. Otherwise it would not be until mid-late May that we would be able to leave.

From March 4 to April 9 it continued to snow. Luckily for us, the weather turned cold for the duration, thus hardening the track for the snowmobile. The 411 remained a challenge—but not as much as it would have been if warmer temperatures had prevailed.

April 9: D-Day

It was cold, snowing and blowing. The track was excellent. When I had finished transporting the last of the boxes and bags to the truck, I returned for the last run, the one in which Jeanne and Scooter, in her carrier, would ride in the sled and be pulled by the snowmobile to the truck. I laid one tarpaulin along the bottom of the sled, then two layers of sleeping bags with two blankets ready to cover the passengers and another tarpaulin to tuck them in. But I made one mistake: I should have arranged it so that Jeanne and Scooter would be facing backwards.

Once we were going, I quickly realized that they were being showered with the snow thrown up by the track of the machine. I stopped. Jeanne said, "Keep going. We'll make it." She pulled the tarpaulin over her head and Scooter's carrier, and on we went.

Roch and his grandson, David, were at Le Relais to meet and see us safely off. They would also take the snowmobile on Roch's truck to La Tuque for storage. They helped us pack the remaining things in the now fully loaded truck, every nook and cranny stuffed with something, and off we went. The 411 was its usual nasty self, but it let us get to the highway and the rest was plain sailing to Brome.

We turned into our driveway. A pair of pileated woodpeckers flew over the truck as a Welcome Home reception committee. We let Scooter into the house, and without hesitation she proceeded directly to the laundry room where she had always been used to being fed.

We fed her.

We were home.

Scooter, at home in Brome. One happy cat!

Postscript

"Do you miss your cabin?" people ask. "Are you happy to be home?"

The answers, and I speak for both of us, are "Yes." and "Yes."

When we set out for our year in the woods, it never was a question of permanently leaving our home, although that did, as this story relates, later enter into our discussions. It was simply a question of spending a year in the woods—which, for reasons I've now explained, became three. At no time during the odyssey did we ever say, "This is too difficult" or "This is too dangerous" or "I want to go home." Nothing obliged us to stay in the woods. We stayed there because we loved being there. The experience far surpassed our expectations both as to the rewards of the physical aspects of the adventure and the human aspects of meeting such marvelous and welcoming people in the communities of La Tuque and Lac-Édouard.

We will go back regularly to stay in our cabin and renew our friendships and acquaintances. And when it is time to go home, I expect that Jeanne will cry.

Recipes

Jeanne's Moose Stew

Combine in a heavy casserole or Dutch oven:

2 pounds (approx. 1 kilo) moose meat, cut in 1" (2.5 cm) cubes

1 large onion, chopped

1 can condensed French onion soup

1 can condensed cream of mushroom soup

1–2 cups (250–500 ml) sliced mushrooms

½ cup (125 ml) dry red wine

Seasoning: 1 bay leaf, 1 teaspoon (5 ml) juniper berries, salt and pepper to taste

Cook, covered, on top of woodstove at low heat for two hours, stirring from time to time. Stew is done when meat is tender. If you wish to thicken the stew sauce, mix ½ cup (125 ml) of flour and 1 cup (250 ml) water. Add to the stew at this point and cook until thickened. Serve on cooked rice or wide noodles.

Vegetables can be added to the basic stew combination: e.g., chopped tomatoes, carrots, turnip.

Oatmeal Bread (2 loaves)

FROM MY VERMONT FRIEND SUE GALLAGHER

Combine in a large bowl:

1 cup (250 ml) oats

1 cup (250 ml) boiling water

¼ (60 ml) cup molasses

2 teaspoons (10 ml) salt

1 cup (250 ml) tap water (additional)

Combine in a separate bowl:

1 (15 ml) tablespoon yeast

¼ cup (60 ml) lukewarm water (110°F/43°C)

Combine ingredients in first bowl with activated yeast in second bowl.

Prepare flour mixture:

5½–6 cups (5½–6 × 250 ml) flour (I use equal parts whole wheat flour and white bread flour.)

Put flour mixture in Cuisinart. Put oat/yeast mixture on top of the flour mixture. Mix.★ Let rise twice in Cuisinart bowl (i.e. until doubled). Put dough in two regular-sized bread pans and let rise a third time.

Bake in oven at 350°F (180°C) for 35 minutes.

★Of course, I did this by hand.

Partridge with Cabbage

FROM MY LA TUQUE FRIEND NATHALIE BERGERON

Ingredients:

2 partridges

8 ounces (250 g) salt pork

2 large onions

1 medium cabbage

flour (enough to cover partridge)

chicken stock

1 teaspoon (5 ml) summer savory

salt and pepper, to taste

Cut the salt pork in cubes and cook them in a pot until they are golden. Remove and set aside.

Cover the partridge with flour, with salt and pepper to taste. Cook the floured partridges in the lard fat until golden. Remove them from the pot and set aside.

Cut the cabbage and the onions in large chunks, add to lard in pot and cook until softened. Leave in pot.

Make two holes in the cabbage/onion mixture and add the partridges so that they are covered by the vegetables. Add chicken stock to have 3 inches (8 cm) in the pot. Add savory and the cooked salt pork cubes.

Cover the pot and cook in the oven at 350°F (180°C) for about two hours or until the partridges are completely cooked.

Denis Trépanier's Marinade for Partridge Brochette
FROM LAC-ÉDOUARD

⅓ cup (80 ml) oil
⅓ cup (80 ml) margarine or butter (I use margarine)
⅓ cup (80 ml) fresh lemon juice
1 garlic clove, chopped
A few sprigs of thyme (use dried thyme if necessary)
Salt and freshly ground pepper, to taste

Whisk together all ingredients. Cut the partridge breasts into cubes and add to the marinade. Marinate in the refrigerator for a maximum of 24 hours (if longer, the meat will taste too lemony).

Reduce the amount of juice to ¼ cup (75 ml) if you wish. You can also add vegetables and onions to the marinade for extra flavour.

Wild Mushrooms (such as Lobster Mushrooms)
from my Lac-Édouard friend Véronique Hallé

It's difficult for me to write down a recipe, as I always improvise and never measure anything. My palate is my trusted guide. But I'll try with a very simple recipe I learned when I worked in a gourmet restaurant, La Fenouillière in Quebec City.

Pasta alla Papalina with Wild Mushrooms

1 medium onion, minced

¾ cup (180 ml) side bacon, cut into ¼-inch (0.6 cm) sticks (you can use regular sliced bacon, but the dish will be fattier)

1½ cups (375 ml) mixed seasonal mushrooms (oyster mushrooms give the sauce a lovely peach colour)

1 clove garlic, minced

3 tablespoons (45 ml) butter (preferably unsalted because of the high salt content of bacon)

3 tablespoons (45 ml) flour

1½ cups (375 ml) milk, heated (do not boil)

35 percent cream, to taste

Salt and freshly ground pepper, to taste

Hydrate the mushrooms in boiling water for about 30 minutes. Meanwhile, in a saucepan, cook the bacon, remove, and reserve. Add the onions to the bacon fat and cook until tender. Put the bacon back in the pan.

Using a fine sieve, strain the mushrooms over a bowl and put aside. Add a piece of cheesecloth and strain the liquid to remove all grit. Add the mushrooms and garlic to the mixture, and cook, stirring occasionally until the mushrooms are tender. Add fat if needed, since mushrooms tend to be highly absorbent. Deglaze the pan with the mushroom liquid, using enough to scrape all the flavourful brown bits from the bottom. Add salt and pepper to taste.

In a separate pan, prepare the béchamel sauce. Heat the butter over medium-low heat until melted. Add the flour, and whisk until the butter totally absorbs the flour and the roux turns a light, golden sandy colour. Whisking constantly, slowly add the warm milk until the mixture is smooth. As soon as it begins to thicken, add the cooked ingredients.

Lower the heat and simmer for about 10 minutes, until the flavours have blended. Thin with warm cream or milk if needed. Adjust seasoning. Serve over your favourite pasta.

Tips for Cooking with Dehydrated Mushrooms

- When you sauté the onions and bacon, add the garlic just before the end of cooking. This way, it will release all its flavors while the preparation is simmering. Otherwise, it will burn and become bitter.

- Meanwhile, rehydrate the mushrooms in boiling water. Once they are hydrated, drain them in a fine sieve placed over a bowl. Reserve the mushrooms. Add a piece of cheese-cloth in the sieve and strain the liquid again. Reserve. Cook the mushrooms and garlic in the onion and bacon mixture, stirring occasionally until tender. Deglaze with the reserved mushroom liquid.

- When using dried mushrooms, I like to cook them with a fresh variety like button mushrooms.

- When fresh and wild mushrooms are dried, rehydrated, and cooked, their flavour is altered. So my friend Louise taught me a new way to preserve them: Clean the mushrooms well, cut them up, and sauté them in butter or olive oil, adding a bit of chopped parsley. Cook until 90–95 percent done and let cool completely. Sort out the mushrooms by type or mix them to taste, and pack in small airtight freezer bags in whatever quantity you wish. Freeze. When you need them, thaw them and finish the cooking. They will taste just as good as if you had just picked them. But do not freeze fresh mushrooms without cooking them first; otherwise they may become bitter.

Blueberry Cake
The Country Kitchen—Old and New

½ cup (125 ml) butter
1 cup (250 ml) sugar
2 eggs, beaten
¾ cup (180 ml) milk
2 cups (500 ml) sifted all-purpose flour
2 teaspoons (10 ml) baking powder
1 tablespoon (15 ml) lemon juice
1 cup (250 ml) blueberries
¾ cup (180 ml) brown sugar
¼ teaspoon (1.25 ml) cinnamon

Cream butter and sugar. Add beaten eggs. Sift dry ingredients and add alternately with milk. Add lemon and fold in berries last. Put in a greased 9" × 9" (23 cm × 23 cm) pan. Mix brown sugar and cinnamon together. Sprinkle on top of mixture. Bake in 350°F (180°C) oven for 35–40 minutes. Serve with heavy cream, ice cream, or a lemon sauce.

Lemon Sauce
Great Dinners from Life

¾ cup (180 ml) sugar
1 tablespoon (15 ml) + 2 teaspoons (10 ml) cornstarch
pinch of salt
1½ cup (375 ml) boiling water
1 teaspoon (5 ml) grated lemon rind
3 tablespoon (45 ml) lemon juice
3 tablespoons (45 ml) butter

In a saucepan, mix the sugar, cornstarch, and salt together. Gradually stir in water. Bring to a boil and cook for 10 minutes, stirring occasionally. Add the lemon rind, lemon juice, and butter. Cook for another minute or two, until the butter is melted and sauce is hot.

Spruce Tips

Spruce tips have been used by indigenous tribes for years. They are full of vitamin C, chlorophyll, and minerals such as potassium and magnesium.

Pick the new green tips in the spring, removing the small brown husk. Freeze them in plastic bags or air-dry them in a dark, well-ventilated room as you would mint leaves. Store the dried tips in airtight jars in a cupboard, out of the sunlight.

Spruce tea can be made from the dried tips. Use them as a substitute for rosemary, add them to soups, or just put a few of them in a glass of water to steep for a while. Or make this spruce tip infusion, as suggested in *The Boreal Feast* by Michele Genest, to be substituted in your favorite fruit jelly recipe. I find *Keeping the Harvest* by Nancy Chioffi and Gretchen Mead very useful for making jams and jellies. (It also has a recipe for making your own pectin from apples and lemons.)

Spruce Tip Infusion for Jelly

Cover 4 cups (1 litre) of spruce tips with water in a medium saucepan and bring to the boil. Reduce heat and simmer for 20 minutes. Cool and refrigerate spruce tips in juice overnight to allow the flavour to fully develop.

Strain into a bowl through a sieve lined with cheesecloth, and then through a coffee filter; this will remove some of the cloudiness from the infusion/juice. You should have about 4 cups (1 litre) of juice. It can be used right away or frozen for later use. Use this juice to make jelly with powdered pectin (see *Keeping the Harvest*, p. 76).

Jeanne's Essential Oil "Pharmacy"

My two sources of oils: Zayat Aroma (www.zayataroma.com) and Coop Coco (www.coopcoco.ca).

Clove — put a drop on gums for relief of pain of a toothache

Eucalyptus — effective against cough and colds: a drop on a cotton ball held under your nose helps relieve nasal congestion

Laurel Noble — a few drops in mixture of Murphy Oil and water for washing floors gives the cabin a wonderful aroma

Lavender — promotes healing and prevents scarring

Lemon — a drop of lemon and a splash of vinegar in the rinsing water for dishes gets rid of any soap and makes dishes sparkle; also good as a toothpaste ingredient

Lemongrass — part of mosquito blend

Myrrh — toothpaste and mouthwash recipe

Peppermint — part of my "mosquito mix"; also deters ants and is good as a toothpaste ingredient

Rosemary — physical and mental stimulant; I love to put a few drops on my fingertips and message my scalp before washing my hair

Spruce, Black — see Laurel Noble

Tea Tree — great antiseptic qualities

Thyme, Red — part of mosquito blend

AND

Origanum — my go-to oil for an oncoming cold or for flu symptoms

Two More Blends
FROM VALERIE ANN WORWOOD's *The Fragrant Pharmacy*

Tooth Powder
1 tablespoon (15 ml) ground, dried orange powder★
1 dessertspoon (10 ml) ground, dried sage
1 dessertspoon (10 ml) bicarbonate of soda (baking soda)
1 teaspoon (5 ml) salt
5 drops lemon essential oil
1 drop peppermint essential oil

If you are having gum problems, add to the above ingredients 15 drops of tincture of myrrh (available at a pharmacy) into which you have added 1 drop of myrrh essential oil. Mix together well in the blender. (I do this with my fingers.)

★ I make my own using rinds, dried in the warming oven of the wood-burning cookstove, from organic oranges. I then grind them finely in a coffee blender.

Mouthwash
A mouthwash can be made by adding 2 drops of essential oil of myrrh to 1 tablespoon (15 ml) of vodka and mixing well. Add only 2 drops of this to each glass of water you use to rinse your mouth.

Making a Pearly Everlasting Wreath

Materials:

Metal crimped wreath ring, 10" (25cm) diameter

Florist's wire

Ribbon for bow

Garden shears for harvesting the flowers

Lots of pearly everlasting with the flowers still closed

A piece of cardboard large enough to lay the finished wreath on to dry the wreath flat

I made my wreath from fresh flowers. (Most instructions call for dried flowers.)

Cut flower clusters with 2–3" (3.5–5 cm) of stem. Gather 3 or 4 clusters together in a tight bunch and wire them firmly to the crimped wire ring. Continue adding clusters, one on the right-hand side of the ring, one on the left, and one in the centre, until the entire ring is generously covered. Place on cardboard to dry flat. Once dry (this takes a week or two), add a bow to the dried flowers and a loop for hanging at the back of the ring.

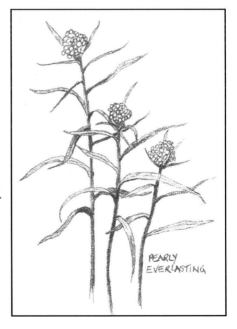

PEARLY EVERLASTING